WHEN CHAINS ARE BROKEN

Jennie Sadler
Romans 10:13

WHEN CHAINS ARE BROKEN

HOW CHRIST SET ME FREE FROM THE CHAINS OF ADDICTION

JENNIE SADLER

Charleston, SC
www.PalmettoPublishing.com

When Chains Are Broken
Copyright © 2021 by Jennie Sadler

All rights reserved
No portion of this book may be reproduced, stored in a retrieval system, or transmitted in any form by any means–electronic, mechanical, photocopy, recording, or other–except for brief quotations in printed reviews, without prior permission of the author.

First Edition

Hardcover ISBN: 978-1-68515-473-8
Paperback ISBN: 978-1-68515-475-2
eBook ISBN: 978-1-68515-474-5

All references to scriptures will be from the New King James Version (NKJV) unless otherwise noted.

DEDICATION

My mom is integral to my story. She, too, was bound by the chains of addiction. She and I used together, but she found freedom in Christ before I did. If it were not for her, I do not know how much longer I would have continued down the destructive road of addiction. In coming alive again through Christ, my mom gave me hope that I, too, could change. Like so many of us who have been bound by the chains of addiction, my mom had a loving heart that was full of good intentions. Addiction is ruthless, however, and it changes us from who God created us to be into someone the enemy needs us to be for his destruction here on Earth. She had ten years of sobriety in 2020 when she graduated on to heaven. The life she lived for God is still a testimony not only to me but to all of those who knew her.

But get up and stand on your feet. For I have appeared to you for this purpose, to appoint you as a servant and a witness of what you have seen and of what I will reveal to you. I will rescue you from the people and from the Gentiles. I now send you to them to open their eyes so they may turn from darkness to light and from the power of Satan to God, that by faith in Me they may receive forgiveness of sins and a share among those who are sanctified.
Acts 26:16–18 (HCSB)

ACKNOWLEDGMENTS

To my family, I thank you for loving me through it all.

To my husband, I thank you for always believing in me. I know without a doubt that you are godsent. Thank you for supporting me on this journey; my heart is forever thankful to be serving Christ with you.

To my beloved mom, I love you and am forever grateful for your prayers. Thank you for being such a bold witness For Christ and not only telling me Who set you free but also for showing me what a life of freedom looks like. Your salvation was and is a beacon of light for me and many others. I look forward to the day I am reunited with you in heaven.

To God, my Heavenly Father, Jesus, my Savior, and Holy Spirit, my teacher, and comforter. Heavenly Father, thank you for loving us so much that you were willing to send us your only son. Jesus, I thank you for paying a debt that I could not pay. Holy Spirit, I thank you for teaching me how to grow closer to God and for empowering me daily to grow in the image of Christ.

TABLE OF CONTENTS

PROLOGUE	XIII
INTRODUCTION	1
A CRY OUT TO GOD	4
HOW IT ALL STARTED	10
ADDICTED	17
A WHOLE NEW REALM	25
LIFE IN THE CITY	34
IDOLATRY	46
THE TRUTH ABOUT ADDICTION	52
STOLEN AND ARRESTED	55
FAILED ATTEMPTS TO CHANGE	62
SOBRIETY OR PRISON	74
PART II: LIVING IN CHRIST & LEARNING A NEW WAY OF LIFE	91
GROWING IN GOD	93
JESUS DIED FOR US ALL	103
WHERE TO BEGIN	110
THE JOURNEY	116
MADE FOR VICTORY	130
I STRIVE TO MOVE FORWARD	140
CONCLUDING PRAYERS	144
ABOUT THE AUTHOR	153

PROLOGUE

Due to years of hidden drug abuse, at the age of twenty-two, I found myself facing years of prison time. I loved my family dearly, yet I had hurt and disappointed every one of them. They had lost all hope in me ever getting straight. I had dreams for a future but was so far away from accomplishing anything. I felt as if the world was against me, and with every turn that I made there, I was facing yet another dead end. I disappointed my loved ones daily. I would not stick with a job. I could not stop getting arrested. I could not stop failing. I fought against the world with the raging and unquenchable desire to use until I had almost lost everything, including my life.

Finally, one day, at the end of my rope, after I had gone as far as the court system was going to let me go, I was given a choice: prison or sobriety—years behind bars or two years in a court-appointed rehab program called Drug Court. I felt like everyone around me was forcing me to change the one thing I liked most about my life: drugs. And truth be told, that is exactly what was happening but this seemingly dead-end road led me to God in a way I could never have imagined. When I accidentally found God in my court-appointed sobriety, I discovered that life was something that could not only be handled with a sober mind but also enjoyed. I found that there is real meaning to life and that there has been all along. I went from living for drugs to living for God. Please join me through this journey of how God opened my eyes and then set me free from the bondage of addiction.

INTRODUCTION

The vision that the Lord has given me is to reach people who are hurting due to the bondage and repercussions of drug abuse—to reach anyone who is going down the same path that I went down. This book is for anyone who is in prison physically and for anyone in prison emotionally and spiritually because of the ever-continuous cycle of addiction. To those of you who are battling this fierce beast, I hear you. I understand you. And I want you to know that you can find a way out of addiction's grips and step out far more ahead in life than you have ever been and farther than you ever could have imagined.

Our God is a God of restoration. Jesus tells us "The thief does not come except to steal, and to kill, and to destroy. I have come that they may have life, and that they may have it more abundantly" (John 10:10). Drugs and alcohol are common tools that Satan, the thief, uses to steal, kill, and destroy homes, families, and lives. Addiction is not partial; it does not care who you are or how you were raised. Satan will inflict its ills upon anyone to do his bidding.

I pray that this book will reach a variety of different lives in various circumstances, so I want to express something. How we became addicted and how circumstances brought us to where we are now will all be different. Some of us were, in fact, raised in a church, and some of us were not. Some of us were raised by parents who sold drugs, and that may have been all that we ever knew growing up. Some of us were taught better than to go near drugs but did so despite better teaching. We are all different, and our lives are different, but our addiction is where we are not different. Rock bottom is rock bottom. Period. If anyone has lost anything due to addiction, then I feel like that person is capable of understanding the pain that we all know too well no matter what his background because ultimately hitting rock bottom is coming to a place of brokenness due to a life of drug abuse.

If you are reading this, perhaps you are seeking answers, help, or a new direction. I am here to share my story, and I pray that it can give you hope because we all can have the freedom in our souls that Jesus Christ has provided for us. And we all can have the love of our Heavenly Father.

As I speak of addiction or refer to addiction throughout this book, I will not call it a disease. I do not believe addiction is a disease, as some are taught. Instead, I believe that addiction is the by-product of sin. Drugs and alcohol are nothing but tools that Satan uses to bind God's children, and addiction is the result. When I was actively using without the ability or desire to quit, I was bound by it, and I was an addict. But once I came to know Jesus Christ as my personal Lord and Savior, I was set free.

Stand fast therefore in the liberty by which Christ has made us free, and do not be entangled again with the yoke of bondage.
Galatians 5:1

God's word says to be quick to stand firm in the freedom that Christ made for us, and because we are free, we must make sure not to entangle ourselves once more with the things from which He set us free.

I have heard it said to label yourself as an addict because you will never be able to use mind-altering substances and live a functioning life successfully, and if you remember that you are an addict by labeling yourself as one, then you will not forget all of the things that drugs and alcohol stole from your life (and will therefore not be tempted to use again). Although not forgetting all that drugs have stolen from us can be significant, I'm afraid I have to disagree with labeling oneself an addict.

God tells us in 2 Corinthians 5:17 (KJV): "Therefore if any man be in Christ, he is a new creature: old things are passed away; behold, all things are become new." So once I accepted Jesus into my life, I was set free from the chains of addiction and newly created in Christ, and God no longer saw me as the addict I had been for so long.

As I have sought to follow God from that day on, I have remained liberated and new. I am not an addict today. I am God's child. If God calls me free and new, then who am I to label myself differently? Now, do I feel like I can get high today and not be bound by drugs as before? No, I know for a fact if I used today that it would ensnare me just as bad today as it did then. But as long as I am not going back to those things that entangled me before, then I am still set free. The difference between those who teach that it is a disease to what I am teaching you now is that they go by the world's understanding. I am teaching from the Word of God that is unfailing and never changing.

The grass withers, the flower fades, But the word of our God stands forever.
Isaiah 40:8

Heaven and earth will pass away, but My words will by no means pass away.
Matthew 24:35

Since God's word is unfailing, it is a solid foundation to stand upon and essential to use as a guide to help one grow in their new life in Christ. Therefore, I will be sharing these truths and how I discovered them as I found God and was set free from the chains of addiction.

A CRY OUT TO GOD

One thing that I cannot fathom in my mind is how gloriously our Heavenly Father can turn what we know as the darkest moments in our lives into something that can further His Kingdom for good. If we are willing to let Him, God will take everything the enemy meant to ruin our lives and use it for His glory. I will not deny the reality that some of the things that I experienced and endured during my drug abuse were some of the darkest times of my life. But as I look back today, my heart is nothing but thankful that I was able to come out on top through His saving grace so that I may be able to give others hope toward freedom.

I will never forget the day that brought me to God. Although my testimony is not a miraculous direct light that appeared down from heaven, effecting instantaneous deliverance, it all happened just like it needed to happen. My boyfriend, whom we will call Jay, and I were out all day driving around while he did his usual thing—dealing drugs. It was a typical day of hustling drugs and whatever else he had, and I had been tagging along riding in the passenger seat as usual. I loved him, and I was good at pretending I did not know or care that he cheated on me. Somehow, I felt that it would not be possible for him to hurt me if I did not let it get to me. I know that the drugs played a significant role in numbing the reality that he was not faithful to me. I tried my best to be strong for myself, and I treated him my best hoping that I could win his heart over to me and only me. But his paranoia had reached an all-time high, and instead of just skipping off for a few hours, he began making me stay by his side at all times. At first, I was okay with it because while he was watching me, I was confident that he was not cheating on me. In the most twisted way, I felt like it was a win-win situation.

But there were many times, like this particular night, when I wanted nothing more than just to go home, but he would repeatedly convince me that we would go home soon. The day had finally become dark, and he promised me this next house would be the last stop. The house we stopped at was the drug dealer's house, which was not out of the ordinary, but that night I noticed an unfamiliar car parked in the driveway. As Jay started to get out, he told me to stay put. I looked at him suspiciously, but he assured me that it would not take very long. As Jay was walking to the front door, a girl got out of the unfamiliar vehicle and met up with him, and they went into the house together. I was immediately upset about it, but I also knew better than to go acting like a madwoman at the dealer's house. So I sat back and tried telling myself that he would not be very long and that I was imagining things, but in my heart, I knew that that was not the case. If you are at all familiar with the life of a drug dealer, him dealing with a random woman was not uncommon, and him asking me to stay behind was not all that uncommon either. I know plenty of times it was for my safety. But what was not normal was that he told me to stay in the car while he went along with another woman.

I honestly cannot tell you how long I sat in that car, but it felt like forever. The longer I sat there, the more reality hit me. I asked myself, "Jennie, what are you doing? Why are you sitting out here like an idiot?" I started feeling deep in my heart, "You don't have to live this way." I know today that it was Jesus speaking to my heart and directing me toward repentance, but I had no clue at the time. The longer I sat there, the harder the impression was until I could not deny it anymore, and I finally broke. I felt it so hard in my spirit, and I had no clue why I was putting up with this kind of treatment when I had a better way of life back home. I had a family who loved me, a future that I could be pursuing, and a different all-around way of living somewhere else. But I was too busy chasing a high to numb myself from feeling any emotion that I was letting the drugs, myself, and another person completely ruin all that I was. It was there in the passenger seat of my 2008 Ford Escape that my eyes became opened to the reality that I had sold my soul to Satan for a high, and I realized I needed to get out, but I had no clue where to start.

    I looked at the keyless ignition and realized I could not even take my own car. Then I looked outside at the dark streets of South Side Oklahoma City, and it terrified me to even think of trying to take off walking. I looked at the dealer's house and knew going in there would not be a good idea either. I already knew that I could not call my family for help because that would give me away, and they would know I was up to no good. Because at that time, no one in my family knew how deep I was into drugs. I thought about all my friends I had closed the door on and the bridges I had burned because of my drug abuse and the drama that came along with it, and I was too ashamed to call them. I was looking in every direction I could think of, but I was not seeing a way out. That is when I realized the tight corner that I had placed myself in. I had no way out, but something told me that I needed to stop living this way. I reclined my seat back as far as it would go so that no one could see me. I started crying uncontrollably because I just knew that God was the only option I had left, but I felt shameful and unworthy to even cry out to the One I had forsaken years ago to live my life the way I wanted to.

    I had last called out to God as a young child. I had been so adamant about ignoring His existence that up to that point, I had not even thought to call out to Him. I did not want to acknowledge that the life I was living would take me to hell. I felt that if I did not acknowledge God and His existence, my lifestyle would not take me to hell. Because if God was not real, then hell was not either. But the longer I sat there, the more I realized that He really was my only hope. I was miserable, I was tired, and I needed something different in life. Finally, I broke and I called out to God and I begged God to save me. I begged Him to please put life back inside of me because I could not take it anymore. I begged Him to show me how to get out of the mess I was in and to take me back home. I continued to cry out, praying for the strength to do what I needed to so that I could get back to my family who loved me and could help me.

I laid in that seat and cried out to the Heavenly Father until I had no more tears to shed, and suddenly a peace came over me. Then, finally, I was able to gain my composure, and I sat up in the seat with an overwhelming desire to call my dad to tell him I was ready to come home.

It was sometime in the middle of the night, so he immediately sounded worried when he answered. I told him everything was okay, but I was just homesick and needed to hear his voice. But he kept questioning me about what was going on. He knew something was off. I finally told him, "I need to come home, Dad. I can't live in the city anymore." I told him that if I did not make it home with my things by next week, he needed to come physically and get me and my things and take me home. And as far as I remember it, that was all of the conversation. Just as I ended the conversation with my dad, I noticed Jay was finally making his way back to the car, and I acted as if nothing had happened. I did not even question him about spending hours inside the dealer's house with another girl. I just sat in the seat quietly, listening to his excuses as to what took so long and his fake apology. I felt in my heart that change was coming, and for the first time in a while, I had a moment of peace.

All the way home, my mind raced from scenario to scenario to scenario. I had no clue what my future held. I just knew I was ready for a change, but peace only lasts so long when you're getting high. Finally, we made it back to my apartment, and Jay pulled out the new sack of crystal and loaded the pipe. Even though I had just cried out for God's help, I took a hit. And then I took another hit. I never said I wanted to stop getting high. I just needed help getting my life back in order. And from there on, we went about our business. It was as if nothing had happened. We got along like most days and went back to laughing, dealing, using, back into the daily hustle of getting high.

The sack that he had just picked up must have been some good meth because after I got high, an entire week went by, and I had not once recalled the moment that I had called out to God, nor did I remember asking my dad to come and bring me home. Little did I know at the time that God knew what was best for me, and even though I did not see any immediate physical changes or feel any lasting spiritual changes in my life, it did not mean that God was not working behind the scenes.

We continued about our everyday business throughout that next week, never slowing down as usual, and believe it or not, since that night, things were going pretty well between us. We were getting along and laughing, and everything was going great. Then one early afternoon, my sister Kristel called me on my cell, and I thought it was strange. So I quickly answered, and she said, "Jennie, where are you?" I told her we were out running errands, and she said, "I need you to get to your apartment and let us inside so that we can start loading up your things." For a moment, I was confused, and I had no clue what she was saying. Then she reminded me of the call I made to my dad the previous week, and my heart immediately dropped. I did not remember making that phone call until she reminded me. I do not know how I forgot it, but I did, and they were there to pick me up, just like I asked them to.

I did not see it then when it happened, but I know that after I called out to God that night, He is the reason I called my dad and told him to come and pick me up. I was the one who called and spoke the words, but it was like God had worked through me and had given me the strength and the ability to do what I needed to. God is so amazing that He will provide us with what we need as our desperate heart cries out to Him. Because when I cried out to Him,

I had a sincere heart cry, and God our Father heard that cry just as a parent hears a child crying out in need. I was not ready for the turn my life was fixing to make by crying out to God. But even as a parent often knows what is best for a child's well-being, God knows what is best for us, and He was there to rescue me from the enemy's trap and my own self-destruction.

HOW IT ALL STARTED

I had not always lived a life of drug abuse—nothing anywhere near it. I was not even raised to participate in any of the things in which I had involved myself. I grew up in a small community in Western Oklahoma where there is nothing but fields and pastures. My mom had three girls. I am the youngest of the three. Even though I had siblings, I am my dad's only child; my parents divorced when I was around one, so I never knew it any other way. I was fortunate that they remained living close enough that I could go to each of their houses as I pleased throughout the week and still be close enough to my school.

I grew up knowing that my family loved me; my mom and dad worked together, raising me the best they could, and I felt secure growing up. My parents were good people with good moral values. I was not raised in the church by my family. But they taught me to be a good, honest person, and I was raised by example. My dad farmed and raised cattle, and my mom always worked a job. I stayed with my dad mostly when I was younger because of my mom having to work. Since my dad worked for himself, he could always take me wherever he needed to go, whereas she couldn't. I always had a special relationship with my dad, and we were closer than my mom and me. But I did not know for the longest time that it was because my mom had an addiction that kept her from me most of the time. I remember hearing rumors about my mom using as a child. I always wondered why it always seemed like she didn't have much time for me, but I still did not know of her secret life until I was in my early teens.

I would go to Wednesday evening services at the local Baptist church with my older sister as a young child. I would occasionally accompany Mema and Papa, my grandparents, to their church. I had a basic understanding that God had sent Jesus, His only son, to die for our sins, but beyond that, I didn't know anything about God.

Eventually, my sister Kristel graduated and moved out, but I still went to Wednesday night services with my friends at another local church. I genuinely enjoyed it, but as I got older, I began to realize that I was the only person in my family, including my siblings and my parents, who was attending church. At this particular time in my life, I did not see my mom much because of her drug abuse. Because Kristel was older, I did not have anyone to watch me at my mom's house, so our visits became less frequent. My heart ached for my mom, and my dad wasn't the churchgoing type. My siblings were just so much older than I, and they had already started their own lives elsewhere. In my young mind, it became burdensome to think of anyone who I loved going to hell. That is when I began to question the actual existence of God. Part of me felt that if He were not real, my loved ones would be safe from hell. However, another part of me wanted God to be real because I thought and hoped that surely there is some kind of life after death because the thought of never living again after death seemed too bizarre for me. I never told anyone the struggle I was having with the reality of God, and I went back and forth in my head for a while.

Then one night after a Wednesday night sermon got to me, I got tired of the relentless back-and-forth battle in my head, and as I went to bed, I prayed to God with desperation. I begged Him to please let me know if He was real, and if He was, I needed Him to show me. I'm not sure what I expected to happen next, but nothing happened immediately. So I just figured that He must not be real and brushed the whole thing off as soon as I awoke the following day. That was the last of that prayer I even remembered until the following Wednesday.

On Wednesday, I went to church as usual. However, on this occasion, as the pastor approached the pulpit to begin his sermon, he paused for a second. Then he finally said, "You know what—I had this message already planned for us today, but this morning God spoke to me and told me that I needed to change my message. God told me to tell all of you that He loves you and that you all needed to hear that He is real and that He does hear your prayer."

I have no idea what my face must have looked like, but the pastor seemed to be looking at me directly. I don't remember anything else about that service because I never got past the fact that somehow, he had addressed everything I had asked God the previous Wednesday night. At first, I was encouraged and filled with awe, but that only lasted through the evening. Once I realized that to have answered me like that God must be real, then I just knew it meant that my family was going to hell if the rapture happened at any moment like the Bible says it will.

So began a vicious cycle in which I would leave Wednesday night services both blessed and encouraged yet sad and discouraged at the same time. At some point, I couldn't take it anymore, and eventually, I stopped going to church altogether. That is the time in my life that I built a wall between God and me. I had this idea that if I would pretend that He was not real to me, then all they say about Him in the Bible was not real to me either. I was unknowingly portraying an ignorance is bliss attitude. Well, I can tell you now that ignorance is not bliss.

I was thirteen years old when I quit going to church and found drugs in my mom's purse for the first time. I had never actually seen or been around drugs before, but I knew enough to know that it was meth I had found. And I knew what people said about drugs—that they were terrible and made you do bad things and stay away from them. My heart was so torn by what I had discovered and all that it meant that I couldn't sleep right for days. I couldn't grasp the cold, hard reality of my mom being a drug addict. When I thought of a drug addict, I thought of a homeless person on the streets or someone who didn't work or have a car. She wasn't a bad person. She didn't do bad things. She was a working adult with a home of her own and a car, just like everyone else, so it made it hard to understand. The kids at school can be horrible, and even my closest friends would tell me how my mom used drugs. I assume it was due to what their parents must have told them. But still, I was angry. My mom had given me the reputation of being the child of a drug user. Because of that, I hated drugs, and I became a little radical about it. Everyone knew I hated drugs because I would let them know. I had made a heartfelt decision that I would never try drugs, and I was sincere about it.

Throughout elementary school, I played basketball, but I never liked it for some reason. But as I came into the sixth grade, I discovered that it was something I was good at, and I started to enjoy it. I thrived at basketball, and I began to love how naturally the game came to me. It was when I entered junior high that basketball became a big part of who I was. My family always encouraged me and supported me—they were always coming to my games. I was on the starting team in junior high, and eventually, in the ninth grade, I played on the high school basketball team starting as well. Playing basketball took up most of my free time after school, which was a good thing.

I always hung out with some of the older kids at school. Most of my friends were juniors and seniors who liked to drink after school and on weekends. So without really thinking anything was wrong with it, I started drinking with them. I had never seen a problem with alcohol because it was legal for adults. I felt like the only issue with alcohol was that I was underage. So I just made sure that I was extra careful to hide it from my family, and if I made sure not to get caught by the cops, everything would be cool.

One night I had plans to stay with my best friend, and we ended up at a party where everyone was drinking. At one point, we were hanging out in the dining room, drinking and watching some of our friends play a card game at the table. Then out of nowhere, I noticed that they were passing a joint around the table. I glanced over sharply at my friend. She just told me to act cool and to ignore it, so I just pretended like all was good like she said. Just as quickly as the joint was lit, it went around the table, and someone put it out. No one even offered it to me, so I never had to turn it down.

Later on, after more drinking, my friend asked if I was ready to go home, and so she and I got in the vehicle with the person who was driving us that night. I assumed we were going home, but we did not go toward her house, so I just figured the plan was to go and ride some back roads for a little bit. The next thing I knew, we were parked in a random pasture. Honestly, I was pretty buzzed, so I was sitting there; I realized that I smelled something burning. I immediately told the driver that he needed to turn the pickup off because I thought the running vehicle had caused the pasture to catch fire. They just started laughing hysterically at what I said, and I realized it was because they had lit the rest of the joint that I had already avoided earlier that night. But I had since then drank quite a bit more than I had consumed earlier when I had first encountered the joint, and I just started laughing with them. Finally, my best friend told me that I didn't have to smoke if I didn't want to but that it was okay and that I could at least try it if I wanted to. I felt differently about it at that moment. It wasn't just that I had been drinking. It was that it had been offered to me by someone I trusted. So I went for it; I smoked the rest of the joint with my friends. The weird part was that I did not feel any different than I was already feeling. I believe that only made me think that weed was not as bad as I grew up believing it was.

They say that marijuana is a gateway drug. I believe it is in some cases, but I believe alcohol is even more so. If I had been in my right mind that night, I would have turned down the joint when it was offered to me the second time because of my moral values. But I didn't because I had been drinking; the alcohol had altered my mind, so it didn't seem like a big deal at the moment. So I tried it, and once I did, I didn't see anything wrong with it. The moment I tried it, I realized how unintimidating weed was, and it was nothing like everyone said. So within the next couple of days, when the opportunity presented itself again, I was cool with doing it again. The second time I tried it was when I got hooked because I had not had any alcohol before I smoked it, and what overcame me was a series of some of the most incredible sensations I had ever felt. It was like my mind was numb to reality. I was in a completely different mindset than I had ever been in before.

The best way I can describe it is that I felt chill, calm, and unmoved by the world around me. Everything that generally bothered me didn't matter at that moment. Marijuana caused me not to care about what people thought, and that was a big deal for me because I was a people pleaser. But the more I used it, the more I was convinced that weed was completely harmless and that anyone who had ever said otherwise was clueless. I felt that just because it messed up someone else's life did not mean it would mess up mine. Even though I was occasionally getting high with my friends after school or on the weekend, I did not feel it changed who I was. I felt like I was still me, and it did not change me into some terrible person. I realized that weed was not scary at all and was the opposite. It was amazing. From that time on, the way I looked at drugs was not the same. Although I still hated the "hard" drugs and wanted nothing to do with anyone who used meth or took pills, the way I looked at marijuana had changed. I had this mindset that all of the other drugs must be the ones that will ruin your life but not weed.

I fully intended to continue life as before, remain who I always had been, and do all the same things I had already been doing. I could smoke weed for fun and still be a successful person. I could keep playing basketball, do well enough in school, and strive toward the bright future I longed for; only now I would be able to do it feeling good. But, unfortunately, even though I did not intentionally plan to make any changes to my life, it was not long before inevitable changes started occurring.

 I began to spend almost all of my spare time with my circle of friends who drank and smoked weed. Changing the people you are around is not something anyone can avoid as it comes with the lifestyle because no one likes to be around someone with whom they cannot be themselves. And even though I was confident that I had not changed, the reality was that I had. My perspective on life had changed. I enjoyed getting high more than anything; not all of my usual friends enjoyed it, so I just spent less and less time with them. I remember this bothering me because I genuinely cared about all the people in my life, but when I got high, I could forget about feeling bad.

 My heart for basketball did not change at first, and it still kept me busy during the week. However, I had started a relationship with someone who hated drugs like I said I did, and for the next three years of high school, I continued living a double life. I was one person with my boyfriend and my family, but with my friends, I was someone else entirely; I felt that this was a good balance for me. This way, I could still participate in socially unacceptable things, like getting high, and no one would know about it. To the outside world, I could look like the same Jennie as always, the Jennie who played basketball, was in a solid relationship, and had plans to attend college for photography after she graduated. All of these things about me were true, but what no one knew was that I hated my emotions. I hated handling them, and the best way to deal with them was to numb them. So everything looked perfectly fine to those outside looking in because I put on a persona that all was well. But on the inside, I longed to get high and stay high so that I would not have to deal with emotions because I felt the most content when I was high.

ADDICTED

I was in the eleventh grade when I started getting high before school, and I couldn't wait until basketball practice was over so that I could get high again. Then there were some days during school that I would come up with an excuse to leave school just long enough to go somewhere and get high. My constant desire to get high put a wedge between my boyfriend and me because I always had to go off somewhere without him to get high. So my increasing drug use started to strain our relationship, which caused frequent disagreements and fights between us.

The fights we got in started as mild arguments but became increasingly toxic. I had to lie about where I was going and who I was going with because I didn't want my boyfriend to know what I was doing. He thought I was cheating on him and would get jealous and angry. We would repeatedly break up and get back together again, but ultimately I could never be loyal enough to choose him over my desire to get high. I wanted to have my cake and eat it too.

I started to wish that he would get high with me. I mean, it was only weed, and I felt like it shouldn't be a problem at all. Then, one day, I felt that if I confessed to him that I had been smoking weed, he would see that weed is not that big of a deal, and he would be okay with me using it and possibly even try it with me. So I told him everything, and I asked him if he would smoke some with me. Well, that idea did not go as planned—he rejected it, and he was not open to the idea of trying it himself and was adamant I quit. That's when things got worse for us because I could no longer get by using behind his back.

In my eyes, I just wanted him to change his concept about weed and accept me for who I was. The thing is, he thought he did accept me for who I was, but he never knew the hidden me, the real me. It was such a tangled mess between my heart for him and my desire to be high. I have always been one with a big heart, and when I love, I love hard. I was faithful to him for most of our relationship because I felt it was morally wrong to cheat on someone. But drugs change your values, and if you have ever used, you most likely know what I am saying. So the fact that I had cheated on him did nothing but add more unwanted emotions.

The summer between my eleventh and twelfth grade was a season of dramatic changes. During that summer, I truly discovered that the longer I stayed high, the better I felt and the less I had to deal with all the stress and self-induced drama that swirled all around me. The more I stayed high, the less I cared about how wrong everything started to look with my boyfriend and friends. I knew something needed to change because things had stopped working as they had before. I knew I had to stop being the person I had become to make things right, but I didn't know how to stop. So I didn't. I just buried myself deeper and deeper into my growing addiction.

Sometime in the middle of my senior year, and due to all the stress I was constantly putting myself in, I was not eating well, and I lost weight. People started saying that I was strung out on meth like my mom, and it hit me hard. I still hated meth and everything about it. I knew what meth could do to a person and a family. I thought everyone knew how I felt about it, and I could not believe people thought I would even go that low.

Then the rumor got to my eldest sister, Tisha, and she reached out to me to see if it was true. She asked me to take a drug test to prove I wasn't lying when I said no. I told her that I would not pass it for marijuana; I took it because I loved my sister and wanted her to believe me, but inside I was angry about the whole ordeal.

Later on, after the drug test I took for my sister, my mom took me to have my senior pictures done. While we were in between sessions and I had to change my outfit, I realized that she had accidentally left her purse in there with me when I locked myself in the changing room. So out of curiosity, I looked to see if she had any drugs, and I found some little baggies with different amounts of crystals in them. So I picked out a baggie with the smallest amount of crystals in it so that she would hopefully not notice it missing. I put the baggie in my pocket and kept it there throughout the rest of that day. As I securely held on to the baggie in my pocket, I kept wondering how I would even use it. Of course, she did not know that I had taken it out of her purse, and I do not think that she ever would have knowingly used meth with me at that time in my life, even if I had asked.

When I got home that evening, I did not even know if it was for sure meth or how to use it. So because I did not have any close friends that used meth, I went to a friend's house and asked her boyfriend, who I knew had used meth before. I knew that he would confirm if it was meth and how to use it if it was. He was excited to confirm when I got there that it was, but he was even more excited to show me how to use it. We did not have any means to smoke it at the moment, so I sat back and watched him as he made a pipe out of a light bulb, black tape, and a straw. I had had enough of rumors and people talking bad about me, and I had a screw-the-world mentality. I figured if I was going to be accused of doing something that I wasn't doing, then I might as well be doing it.

And so, we smoked it, and the crazy thing is I did not even feel a head change. I sat there wondering why I did not feel high because he said that he was pretty high and that it was good stuff, but I was not feeling any different. So I left their house and went to work at the steakhouse that I cooked for part-time. After work, I went home, and I was not tired; I went to my bathroom and hung out there so that no one would know I was still awake. Without anything else to do in a bathroom, I just sat in there and cleaned till three o'clock in the morning. By then, I could go to sleep, but I did not ever feel a head change. I woke up the following day, and I was disappointed in the meth because I could not wrap my head around the idea of it being a "bad drug" if you did not even feel any different after smoking it.

After that night, I spoke with several people about it, and there were quite a few people who told me that they did not feel high the first time they used meth either. I think that is what made me feel like maybe meth was not as bad as people made it out to be either because I had tried it, and it did not change who I was. So at this point, I felt determined to try it again because now I wanted to know what made people want to use it. It was about another week before I had the opportunity to sneak some more out of my mom's purse. I found a night where I was by myself, and this time I did not need to ask for help. I just used the knowledge I had gained and made my pipe out of a light bulb. But this time was different; I felt high, and I was amazed. I was blown away at the energy I suddenly had with hardly any sleep and the incredible confidence it gave me. Meth was not the same as weed. I was relaxed and carefree with weed, but with meth, I felt empowered—like I could do anything, accomplish anything, and no one could stand in my way even if they tried.

Trying to think of words to describe exactly how it made me feel proves to be kind of challenging. But I do remember walking into school feeling like I was determined and that I could accomplish things. How often do we not get something done or feel like not doing it because we are tired and do not have the energy to do it? But on meth, I had plenty of energy, and I was excited to get to basketball practice because I just knew that I could use all of this energy to help me on the court.

I played some of my best games while I was utterly stoned, so I just knew that meth would make my game so much better with all the energy I had. But when it came down to it, and I tried playing basketball high on meth, it was a disaster. I believe that my mind was just in too many places at once. I was all over the place, and it was like my mind was so energized that I could not physically keep up with my mind. It repeatedly proved itself to be a bad idea, so I decided not to attempt to play any more games while I was high on meth. But the thing about addiction is that you never really schedule when, where, and how very well. So I would attempt only to do it on certain days, but then out of nowhere, I would get it offered to me; of course, I would not turn down a free high. So in turn, I would try hard to focus and do my best in the game, but those days became the worst games I ever played. I could not figure out how to make it work. But since it kept happening to me, I started getting frustrated at basketball because I could not play right while I was high on meth. But I desired to be high because it was when I was high that I felt the most content in my mind. I was not used to playing bad games or sitting on the bench. I was trying hard to make it work, but I could tell it was not working out. My game was just off, and that did nothing but discourage me. Then I would be in practice and loath every minute of it because I had my mind on other things. I began to think if I was not good at playing anymore, all I wanted to do was something different. So slowly but inevitably, my heart stopped being in it, and since everything felt so off, I was convinced to quit basketball. I never even allowed myself to regret quitting; I just stayed high, and that made it easier to move on.

The easiest thing for an addict to do is to get high and forget. My life was changing drastically, but I was too blind and unwilling to see how my choices affected my life. I had a new group of friends because not all of my weed-smoking friends were cool with using harder drugs, so I had to eventually isolate myself from them because they did not all understand me anymore. Due to quitting basketball, losing most of my lifelong friends, and constantly fighting with my boyfriend, I felt depressed. I hated going to school because no one there understood me, and the ones who tried to understand me were only concerned about telling me how I was messing up my life. So in turn, I avoided them altogether.

My family didn't know any of this was happening in my life. And I had fallen into a pit of serious depression because of it all. I felt done with school and the people there, so I started skipping school and did not show up for almost an entire week. I easily got away with this behavior without it being noticed immediately because my dad lived thirty minutes away from the school I attended. Because we lived so far away, he had purchased a house in the town that I went to school in as a family home so that I could have a place to stay on the late nights I had from ball games. It was also so that I could have a place to go after school when it was needed. Although it was a family home, it was mostly for my use because he knew I did not need to be staying at my mom's due to her drug abuse. My dad was trying to protect me, but little did he know that I was already sucked into that life. Then after a week of not showing up at school, the superintendent drove by my house and saw me sitting outside, so he pulled into my driveway and expressed his concern for me. He talked to me about starting an alternative-education program to still work toward my high school diploma, but I would not have to continue high school traditionally. I was more thankful than I let on because I did not have a clue what to do. I never wanted to drop out of school, but I did not know how to handle the transition that had taken place in my life.

So I started alternative education for the second semester of my senior year. Because the program was self-paced and I was determined to get out of school, I finished my second semester at least three months before traditional school was over. And while I waited for graduation, I was able to work full time. Things seemed to be looking up, and surprisingly I was not using that much. It was just here and there, and I was trying. I told myself I could still move on and pursue my dreams of becoming a photographer. I thought the people in town and people at the school were the problems in my life. I knew that my life would get so much easier if I could get away from them and their drama.

I found a photography school three hours from my home in Moore that took nine months to complete. My boyfriend did not know that I had started doing harder drugs. I think he felt the absence from my friends had encouraged me to stop smoking weed, so we were getting along pretty well. When the time came, he moved with me to the Moore area so I could complete the photography program, and it was all supposed to be temporary until I finished.

Shortly after we moved, I was inside of a restaurant applying for a job and needed some info from my driver's license, which I had left out in the car in my wallet. My boyfriend was sitting in the car and was waiting for me to finish, so I texted him and asked him to open it up and give me the information. I forgot about the stash of meth I had buried in my wallet because it had been in there for days untouched. As soon as I got back in the car, he threw the bag at me and said, "What's this? Huh? Using meth?" I told him the most famous line of an addict, "The bag's not mine. I was just keeping it for a friend." Of course, he didn't believe me. He started calling me all sorts of ugly, nasty names and ridiculing me for it. So I said ugly things back.

He had already started driving back to the apartment during our fight that was growing more and more intense by the second. The argument intensified as we got closer to my apartment. He was finished listening to my excuses, and as I type this, I can understand why, but at the moment, I was just so desperate for him to hear me. Finally, we pulled into the apartment complex's driveway, and I snapped because my emotions had enough of the names he was calling me. I jumped out of the moving vehicle. I do not know what I was thinking, but I think it was a dumb and desperate attempt to get his attention off of my mess up and to listen to what I had to say. All that my stunt did was skin my legs up pretty badly and make me look like a crazed idiot. There wasn't much to say after we got home. We apologized to each other and spent the rest of the evening mainly in silence. I think that deep down, we both knew that we could not go on like this any longer.

We went to sleep that night telling each other that it would get better; I promised to be finished with drugs, and I meant it. Although I loved him and wanted a life with him, I realized the biggest problem in our relationship was that I used drugs, and he did not like it. Before that day, I had it in my mind to do better and give up most of the drug life. But that night, I realized I needed to give it all up to get everything in life lined up and get back to where I used to be as a person and where we used to be as a couple.

The following day, I had an interview for another job, but I went alone. When I came back, he had a bag packed and some of his things gathered together, and he told me that he had found some work in Kansas shoeing horses. The idea did not seem entirely unrealistic because he had mentioned something similar before, but I did not feel good about the whole idea. I knew something was off. He promised me that it would just be for a week or so, and then he would be back home. He left early that following morning. That same day I got a call back from the job I had applied for to start work waiting tables the next day. So despite everything that had happened, I was still hopeful we could work things out.

I started my job and was staying busy while waiting on him to get back. But after he had been gone for three days, I could not get him to answer his phone anymore. And he wouldn't return my texts. So finally, I started to get concerned, thinking of the worst possible scenario, like he had wrecked, and nobody knew who to contact or that no one even knew that he had wrecked. So I called and called, but there was no answer; I called his parents, and they told me they had not talked to him either. I went this way for a week before I realized how obvious it was as to what had happened. He had left me, and though I deserved it, I was devastated. I felt that he did not understand how hard I was trying to get right in my life, and I think that broke me the most. So I immediately resorted to doing what I knew best whenever I hurt; I got high, stayed high, and took to using as I never had before.

A WHOLE NEW REALM

I was so convinced that I would never have to wake up to reality if I stayed awake, so I refused to go to sleep. If you do not know this already, that was a terrible idea; seven days without sleep is not good for a person's mental health. And up to that point in my life of using, not one person ever told me about shadow people. Wikipedia describes a shadow person as "the perception of a patch of shadow as a living, humanoid figure, and interpreted as the presence of a spirit or other entity by believers in the paranormal or supernatural." Now, to anyone who has ever used meth, a shadow person is something you see when you have stayed up too long and need some sleep. Most people who use or have used joke about the reality of shadow people, but all jokes aside, they are real. The best way to describe a shadow person is to see things or people like figures that are not there. Shadow people are mostly seen in the dark.

The first time I encountered a shadow person was when I was sitting on a bench outside a friend's apartment building and smoking a cigarette. I had been up for seven days, and I was trying to pull through. Two weeks had passed since my boyfriend had last answered his phone. I had so many people in my life trying to help me and encourage me, but the only comfort I wanted would not answer his phone.

I was staying with a friend who was helping me the best she could, all the while supplying most of my drugs. I took some time to go outside alone. I do not remember what time it was, but it was late; I am certain the rest of the world was asleep. As I sat there, looking off into the apartment complex, I suddenly noticed that the trees looked like people were sitting in them. So I started looking into all of the trees around me, and I thought there was no way this was a reality. I thought I must be imagining things because if I looked hard enough, every single tree had a figure in it, sitting and looking down at me or toward me. I did not move but instead sat there and stared back at them. I thought it was bizarre, and I kept wondering how and why I saw things in the trees. I think the strangest part is that I did not get scared and take off running. Because honestly, I was a big chicken. I did not even do dark; I hardly ever had sat in the dark by myself, not to mention sitting in the dark looking directly at what seemed to be people like figures in the trees and not running away from them. This just goes to show how badly drugs alter our minds and our true selves.

The longer I looked at them, the more I knew they were not there physically because they did not look human. I continued to look around, and the figures were everywhere; I just stared back at them and watched them in the same way they seemed to be watching me. Finally, after what seemed like hours, I just got up and went back inside the apartment. The next day I couldn't stop thinking about what I had experienced, so I decided to tell my friend about it. She just laughed and said, "You gotta get some sleep, Jennie."

I know today that what I saw that night was not a joke; it was real. If I take the time to explain this from a biblical perspective, it will be beneficial and shed some light on this subject. Maybe it will make any strange occurrences that one may have had while using drugs clearer to them. I know that it was the case for me when I first came to this revelation of truth.

The deception that drugs place in a person's mind is very real. I will explain to you through biblical examples exactly how deep and involved drug use is in the spiritual realm. Most people do not know how drug use is tied directly to the spiritual realm, and the experience of shadow people is not just a person's mind playing tricks on them. Shadow people are demons, and they are in the spiritual realm. But a natural mind does not usually see the things that are in the spiritual realm. However, at times, God can and will open people's eyes to see into the spiritual realm for His purposes and His glory. For example, we read about Elisha and his servant in 2 Kings.

> *Now the king of Syria was making war again Israel; and he consulted with his servants, saying, "My camp will be in such and such a place." And the man of God sent to the king of Israel, saying, "Beware that you do not pass this place, for the Syrians are coming down there." Then the king of Israel sent someone to the place of which the man of God had told him. Thus he warned him, and he was watchful there, not just once or twice. Therefore the heart of the king of Syria was greatly troubled by this thing; and he called his servants and said to them, "Will you not show me which of us is for the king of Israel?" And one of his servants said, "None, my lord, O king; but Elisha, the prophet who is in Israel, tells the king of Israel the words that you speak in your bedroom." So he said, "Go and see where he is, that I may send and get him." And it was told him, saying, "Surely he is in Dothan." Therefore he sent horses and chariots and a great army there, and they came by night and surrounded the city. And when the servant of the man of God arose early and went out, there was an army, surrounding the city with horses and chariots. And his servant said to him, "Alas, my master! What shall we do?" So he answered, "Do not fear, for those who are with us are more than those who are with them." And Elisha prayed and said, "Lord, I pray, open his eyes that he may see." Then the Lord opened the eyes of the young man, and he saw. And behold, the mountain was full of horses and chariots of fire all around Elisha.*

> *So when the Syrians came down to him, Elisha prayed to the Lord, and said, "Strike this people, I pray, with blindness." And He struck them with blindness according to the word of Elisha. Now Elisha said to them, "This is not the way, nor is this the city. Follow me, and I will bring you to the man whom you seek." But he led them to Samaria. So it was, when they had come to Samaria, that Elisha said. "Lord, open the eyes of these men, that they may see." And the Lord opened their eyes, and they saw; and there they were, inside Samaria! (2 Kings 6:8–20)*

The king of Syria was making war against Israel. Every time the king of Syria made plans to attack from a specific direction, Elisha, the man of God who was given divine revelation from God, would warn the king of Israel of the enemy's plans. Then due to the warning, the enemy's plans would be counteracted, which greatly upset the king of Syria. He was sure that someone from his army was against him and working for the king of Israel because logically, there was no other way that the king of Syria's plans could have been revealed like they were. But one of the king's servants assured him that there was not a spy in their camp but rather a man of God who knew of the plans spoken in secret, and this man of God was the one who revealed them to the king of Israel. This made the king of Syria even more determined to defeat the Israelites, and he chose to get rid of the man of God.

The king of Syria sent for Elisha's location, and once it was determined, he sent horses, chariots, and a great army to surround the city where the man of God was located. When Elisha's servant woke up early and stepped outside, the first thing he saw was that the enemy had them surrounded without any way to escape. Immediately Elisha's servant reacted with fear, exclaiming, "Alas, my master! What shall we do?" The servant was afraid because what he could see in the natural realm was apparent defeat. They were surrounded and found themselves in an apparently helpless situation. But Elisha, being a mighty man of God, was not moved by the enemy's tactic. Elisha walked in the spirit of God, and he was confident of what God was capable of even if it looked like there was no other way in the natural realm. Because Elisha was an anointed and gifted man of God, he could see into the spiritual realm that most people do not know exists. Elisha reacted according to what he could see in the spiritual realm and not what was visible in the natural realm, and he was confident about what God allowed him to see. Whenever Elisha prayed for God to open his servant's eyes so that he may see, God was moved, and He permitted the servant to see into the spiritual realm. This way, he could be encouraged as Elisha was and see what was taking place right before them. The servant saw that even though it looked like the enemy army physically surrounded them, the enemy army was surrounded by God's army. And there were more in God's army than there was in the enemy's army.

This scripture passage confirms that things are going on in a spiritual world all around us that we do not see. We can also read about this in Ephesians 6, where apostle Paul teaches us that we are not fighting a physical battle but rather a spiritual one.

> *For we do not wrestle against flesh and blood, but against principalities, against powers, against the rulers of the darkness of this age, against spiritual hosts of wickedness in the heavenly places.*
> *Ephesians 6:12*

In the verses following this, Apostle Paul stresses the importance of the armor of God that the believer needs to wear to fight effectively. If we do not wear the spiritual armor provided for us, we will not gain victory because we cannot possibly fight a spiritual battle with physical weapons. As we have just read, it is possible to see into the spiritual realm, and it may not be something that we are all gifted to do. But God will allow some people to see things taking place in the spiritual realm, just like He allowed Elisha and his servant, so that they may know how to fight a battle effectively. In Daniel chapters nine and ten, we read how God permitted an angel to appear unto Daniel after Daniel spent time praying and fasting before God concerning His people and His nation. God allowed an angel to speak to Daniel to provide encouragement and understanding.

> *Yes, while I was speaking in prayer, the man Gabriel, whom I had seen in the vision at the beginning, being caused to fly swiftly, reached me about the time of the evening offering. And he informed me, and talked with me, and said, "O Daniel, I have now come forth to give you skill to understand. At the beginning of your supplications the command went out, and I have come to tell you, for you are greatly beloved; therefore, consider the matter, and understand the vision.*
> *Daniel 9:21-23*

> *Then he said to me, "Do not fear, Daniel, for from the first day that you set your heart to understand, and to humble yourself before your God, your words were heard; and I have come because of your words. But the prince of the kingdom of Persia withstood me twenty-one days; and behold, Michael, one of the chief princes, came to help me, for I had been left alone there with the kings of Persia. Now I have come to make you understand what will happen to your people in the latter days. For the vision refers to many days yet to come.*
> *Daniel 10:12-14*

God sent an angel to minister to Daniel, and the scriptures tell us the angel had set out from the first day that Daniel's words were heard but that he had been fighting against the prince of the kingdom of Persia for twenty-one days. This was not any physical battle that he was fighting; this was a spiritual battle going on in the spiritual realm that exists within our earthly realm. Now that the reality of a spiritual realm is established within the word of God, we can learn how this pertains to drug abuse.

Unless God opens a person's eyes to see into the spiritual realm for His purposes, then it is witchcraft. If a person taps into the spiritual realm by their means or through any medium, they are practicing witchcraft. A medium can be described as something in a middle position. I am sure you have heard of mediums for the use of contacting the spirit world. That person is in the middle of the natural realm and spiritual realm. When a person uses a Ouija board, they are serving the purpose as a medium and using the board as a tool to contact the spiritual realm.

Similarly, the person using mind-altering drugs becomes a medium, and the drugs become a tool. God clearly states through His word that witchcraft is forbidden even to the punishment of death.

"Thou shalt not suffer a witch to live" Exodus 22:18 (KJV)

There shall not be found among you anyone who makes his son or his daughter pass through the fire, or one who practices witchcraft, or a soothsayer, or one who interprets omens, or a sorcerer, or one who conjure spells, or a medium, or a spiritist, or one who calls up the dead. For all who do these things are an abomination to the Lord, and because of these abominations the Lord your God drives them out from before you. Deuteronomy 18:10-12

As we can see through the scriptures, God did not take witchcraft lightly. He wants His children to serve Him and only Him (Deuteronomy 6:13-15). Today, drug users do not realize that drugs were initially used to contact the spiritual realm; drugs were a tool for witches, shamans, and pagan priests to reach the spirits they worshiped. And for anyone who uses a mind-altering substance, it opens the door to the enemy and places them in the direct position of a demonic attack. Why else would people who are high be so completely different from who they are when they do not use? Why else would the things that seem unnatural or unappealing to a sober mind all of a sudden seem so natural and appealing to the intoxicated mind? Because the user has unknowingly or knowingly opened the door for demonic spirits to come into their minds and to be a part of their lives. As I have gained this knowledge, it has opened my eyes to the reality of drug abuse. The Old Testament was originally and mostly written in the Hebrew language. The New Testament was originally written in the Greek language. But sometime around the third century, the Old Testament was translated into Greek, known as the Septuagint. So when you study the Bible and the context of scriptures, it is common to look into the original Hebrew or Greek language for a particular word to gain a deeper understanding of what is being said. Because when you translate one language to another, there are sometimes differences, such as one language may not even have a particular word in their vocabulary that another language has.

When you see the word witchcraft in the word of God and look at the Greek word for a deeper understanding of it, the word is *Pharmakia*. Pharmakia means "healing or harmful medicine, a healing or poisonous herb; a drug, poison potion; magic." So when you read Galatians 5:19–21 (KJV), it says, "Now the works of the flesh are manifest, which are these; Adultery, fornication, uncleanness, lasciviousness, idolatry, witchcraft, hatred, variance, emulations, wrath, strife, seditions, heresies, envying's, murders, drunkenness, revellings, and such like: of the which I tell you before, as I have also told you in time past, that they which do such things shall not inherit the kingdom of God." The word witchcraft here was originally Pharmakia that ties into magic and drug use. This example and the ones earlier are not the only places where the Bible mentions the word witchcraft; it is mentioned in the Bible from Exodus to the book of Revelations. I will not go very far into the study of Pharmakia, but it is a fascinating study. If you are interested in it, I have read a book called *Pharmakia* by Robert A. Orem Jr., and he conducts a very in-depth study on the subject. But we have enough knowledge to know that God does not allow witchcraft for His people, and it was and is for a reason!

Witchcraft is full of magic and spells where people either try to be their god or create a god. That is idolatry, and we are to worship no other gods but God alone (Exodus 20:3). I know that most of us never used drugs to contact the spirit realm, but that is why they have been used for centuries. Think about it. There is no logical explanation as to why people become entirely different on drugs than they are off of them. That is because the drug user unknowingly or knowingly opened the door for demonic spirits to come into their minds and to be a part of their lives. As I have gained this knowledge, it has opened my eyes to the reality of drug abuse.

However, I do not think any foreknowledge on this subject would have changed the reality of ever trying drugs for the first time because I am not sure I would have believed it if someone had told me. I did not have enough knowledge of the Bible to have believed it, but I have given you biblical truth along with this revelation; I pray that it can open your eyes to see the truth of drug abuse. It is evil! After my incident with shadow people, my intoxicated mind made a "self-care" rule to always sleep by day three or before. Because I had realized if I went past three days, things got too weird, and I did not care too much to be a part of all that.

LIFE IN THE CITY

So throughout all that I was putting myself through, I am sure my family knew that something was going on with me, but I do not think they could have ever imagined all of the things I involved myself in. Eventually, it was time for my photography classes to start, and I had no desire to go. It was not that I just wanted to give up, but not only was I lost in the daily hustle of staying high, I just had no clue how to start over and put my life back in order.

When it came time, I started classes to please my family and do what I knew needed to be done, but I gave up within two weeks. I quit because it interfered too much with my daily need to get and stay high. I did not realize that was why I had quit at the time. I had just convinced myself that I did not need classes to teach me photography. In all actuality, that is true as a photographer can become successful through self-teaching methods. But the thing is, with an addict's mindset, there is the famous thought, "I will get to it." I had planned to teach myself everything I needed to know; I had even gone to a bookstore and bought a book on photography so that I could teach myself all that I needed to know. But getting high and staying high had become my full-time job, and it took up all of my time, concentration, and motivation. I was always on a mission to get or find, or I always had something to do or somewhere to go that revolved around drugs. There was never time even to try and learn anything because I always told myself I would "get to it."

One evening, a friend and I were trying to buy some meth, but everywhere we went to buy, they were waiting to buy also. We ended up waiting all day long; we waited at so many random people's houses that day, but nothing ever came in. So we ended up having to go outside our usual circle of people to find something. At this time in my addiction, I always knew somebody who knew somebody else who could hook me up with whatever I wanted. But through a series of circumstances that night, I met the drug dealer that everyone was waiting on; his name was Jay. He immediately started hitting on me. I knew better than to go there because I knew drug dealers' lives, and I was not interested in being a part of it. I even thought that he was a little too fancy in his perfectly clean white tennis shoes. But his persistence toward me that night made me feel special, which made it a lot harder to resist. At some point that night, I even discovered that he had a girlfriend. That should have been a red flag, but I didn't pay much attention to it because I had no intention of getting involved with him.

It was sometime after midnight when we finally got what we had been waiting on. We all got high, and then my friend and I bought what we were waiting for all day. When we tried to leave, he insisted that he take me home. I knew that he was trying to figure out where I lived. He insisted on driving me, and I finally gave in. By the time we had made it to my apartment, I had caved in and given him my phone number. On the one hand, I was hoping that he would not call me and move on to the next girl, but on the other hand, I felt it might not hurt to know the guy in case I had another rough night trying to re-up.

A week went by before he called me, but when he did call, he asked if he could drop by my apartment to get high. It became a routine that he would come by at least once a day and get me high and would leave. We continued to meet up for a while, and I would continue to buy drugs from him; while I knew he had a girlfriend, he never did bring her to my apartment. Within a couple of months, he and his girlfriend broke up, and we started seeing each other officially. I would never have imagined the journey to come. Today

I do not hesitate to call it the most traumatizing chapter of my life. There were many things that I had to be set free from and healed from due to this relationship. As I type this, I am praising God for His healing power that has set me free, and I share this chapter of my life willingly because I want others to know the things that they too can overcome and how God can use the most painful parts of their past for His glory.

My relationship with him did not start badly at all—it was terrific. I was adored and showered with random gifts, although I know now that they were from people who randomly traded anything they could to get drugs, and unfortunately, most of it was probably stolen. Plus, he always had the drugs I wanted, and I never had to search for them. At first, I kept my life completely separate from his life of hustling. I would see him at my apartment throughout the day and night, but I never went with him to make any kind of drug deals. I was not ever really interested in going with him either. I was content to be high and do my own thing with my small group of people.

Of course, there were some sketchy signs and red flags about many things he did, but my heart craved someone to love me so badly that I chose to ignore it. The life that he was used to living was so unlike anything that I had ever lived or seen. As I have already mentioned, I was born and raised in a small community, and all I knew was the way of country life. The life that I was used to was farm life, where everyone knew everyone. It was a place where everybody waved at each other when they met on the road. I would go as far as to say that most people even recognized who drove what vehicle. The school that I attended until I was a junior had less than one hundred students in it, and it was not uncommon for every boy in the school to have a knife in their pocket and a gun in their truck. This is because almost everyone there was a farmer or rancher, and they were work necessities. Not one person ever threatened someone with them either.

The small town I lived in could be cruel as far as rumors and everyone knowing or thinking they knew your business. But looking at the bigger picture, the small community I was from was full of friendly people who genuinely cared about helping someone in need. Then here I was in the middle of a city where life wasn't even close to that. People didn't wave, and if you did, it was awkward or scary. People were in their own world, doing their own thing. Also, it was so big that there were drug dealers, gangs, and cartels, just like in the movies. I had no knowledge that these things existed. I guess it would be safe to say that I was experiencing culture shock.

I even started to understand and relate to hip-hop music because the songs seemed to be about my life. I have always had a heart for music, and I have always loved a good, meaningful song, but I could never understand hip-hop. Even though I lived in the country, I could barely handle country music because I did not much relate to it. I loved rock music—anything with an electric guitar and some deep lyrics. So before I moved to the city, my musical style glorified the life I loved, which was drugs and rock and roll because rock and roll somehow always touched base with my sad, broken spirit and do-not-care attitude. But then, when my life had changed to a whole new scene, I understood hip-hop and rap on a new level, and the songs related to my life of drugs, drug deals, drug dealers, and living the reality of a previously hidden world.

Little by little, I was conforming to that lifestyle. One compromise at a time, I was changing from who I was into who I needed to be to survive and thrive in the world in which I had surrounded myself. At first, a big part of me enjoyed this new fast-paced city life, but the other part of me was not quite sure about it; there were times when I was completely freaking out on the inside.

My parents did not raise me to live the life of a drug dealer, and I knew better. My dad taught me by example to work hard for the things I want—not take everything I desire. I was taught to work for money—not sell drugs for it. So I never grew comfortable with the idea of selling drugs, and it was not something I did much. I always preferred to buy my drugs and work to support my habit. But I was more than willing to surround myself with people who knew no other way of living than to sell drugs.

I purposefully kept it where I did not even know half of the things going on in the drug-dealing world because everyone that knew me knew I was not all about it. I was so brand new to the entire lifestyle that I had acquired the nickname "Brand New." In most places I went, people called me by that name. They were just as intrigued by me not knowing anything about that lifestyle as I was. Although brand new is what I was, being brand new also was my biggest drawback. My naive mind trusted people until they proved differently, but I had to learn that I should have done it the other way around and not trusted anyone until they proved trustworthy to me.

Once Jay came home with a little Ford Ranger pickup that he said he bought from someone, which was not uncommon in his line of business. I was always so shocked by the things people give up just for more drugs. But he was using a screwdriver to start it, so I asked him what was up with that. He just told me that the steering column had messed up, and the previous owner had to use a screwdriver to start it. I am rolling my eyes as I type this. I thought it sounded strange, but I just shrugged it off and gave him the benefit of the doubt.

There was another time when he took me to a neighborhood in the middle of the night to pick up a car. The house we went to had no lights on, so the people were either asleep or not home; he told me that he paid for the car, and the people he bought it from expected him to pick it up. So he got in the car and started it and then asked me to drive it home for him. I did not think anything of it and just did as he asked. But as I was driving it to the apartment, I noticed that the ignition switch was messed up, and right there, on the floor, was a screwdriver. I realized that something was not right. As soon as we got to the apartment, I unleashed on him because I realized that I had just stolen a car. He tried to assure me that I had not, but I knew better that time; I decided not to listen to him the next time he needed me to drive a car. Incidents like this are precisely why I got that nickname.

Despite my efforts to stay separated from the activities I surrounded myself in, I just couldn't. Little by little, I was starting to be dragged deeper into the lifestyle of a drug dealer's girlfriend, and before I knew it, I was in too deep. One of the biggest shocks that I had experienced during my stay in the city happened on my dad's birthday, and it could not have happened at a worse time.

My dad's birthday is on Christmas Eve, so traditionally, every year, our small town has a community Christmas that had been going on for almost a century at the time. My dad grew up attending this Christmas pageant, and so did I. We would go on Christmas Eve, his birthday, and we would always go to a family friend's house afterward and eat supper with them and then go home. Well, even though I was in the midst of this new life that no one knew about, I still had not forgotten my roots. The drugs had not completely taken over who I was because I not only desired to go but genuinely looked forward to going.

There was never a part of me that did not desire to see my family or be around them. I just never seemed to get to it. In my addiction, getting high was my first and only priority, and I just put everyone and everything else in my life on the back burner. I would always make plans to go see them, but if you are not familiar with "plans" in the drug world, they constantly get wrecked. They get wrecked even more than you can imagine. Just imagine with me for a second; it is kind of like the reality of how plans do not always work out due to life, people, and circumstances. But then add the fact that every person involved in it is completely unreliable and sketchy. In the drug world, there is always somebody somewhere at all times trying to trip you up purposefully. There is always somebody plotting to steal your drugs, money, or possessions so that they can sell them to buy more drugs. It is a dog-eat-dog world. So due to my lifestyle and the fact that my happiness depended on unreliable people and resources, it was like a domino effect, and I became unreliable. I would always tell my family that I was coming to visit and then never show up. It would always worry them because I was not raised to say I would do something and then not do it. It would always bring up a lot of questions, and they always had a lot of concerns. So I just stopped saying I was even coming at all. But because it was a holiday, I made it a priority to go home and see my family. I wanted to see my dad and spend time with him, and more than that, I wanted Jay to go with me and meet my dad and enjoy a normal Christmas tradition.

My boyfriend agreed to go, and I was so excited. We got ready that day at a decent time, and when we left the apartment, we had planned to make one stop and meet up with someone across town to smoke a blunt before the drive so that we could be calm and collected during the visit. I had no clue who we were meeting until we pulled up next to them at a store. The moment I saw who it was, I had an uneasy feeling in my stomach. I had always believed that if someone was my enemy or did me wrong, I should not have anything to do with them. I mean, why put yourself in a situation in which someone can hurt you worse or make you miserable? But that person had weed, and we did not; so Jay went for it. I was uneasy about allowing this person in the car with us that morning, but Jay always had this mentality to keep his enemies close to him.

The girl we met up with had another girl with her whom neither of us knew. They got in my car, and we drove around some neighborhoods and got high. After we were all really stoned, the girl neither of us knew asked us to take her somewhere to buy some cigarettes. But when Jay went to pull into a store, she claimed that not all of the stores had the kind she wanted and then asked us to take her to a specific location. I felt uneasy about the whole situation, especially since we needed to get going, and this girl seemed to keep us from moving on. But I just sat in the passenger seat and kept my mouth shut, mostly because at that time, I was too afraid to speak up. Every place she asked us to go to, Jay noticed someone near the parking lot he wanted to avoid. He would say, "No, I'm not stopping here; I see [so-and-so]." When I asked him who that was, he would tell me that they could not be around each other. I kept wondering who he was avoiding, and I thought these guys must be real enemies because here we are hanging around this person he did not trust or "like to be around" either. Before we made an actual stop, we ended up driving across the city from the north side to the south side.

Considering we saw this guy that Jay was avoiding everywhere we went should have been a big red flag, but the girl finally convinced Jay to stop at a Walmart. Mind you, this was on Christmas Eve, and the parking lot was overly crowded with people buying last-minute gifts and shopping for the holidays. We dropped them off near the front door of Walmart, and then as Jay was putting the car in drive to go and find a place to park, he realized that he was trapped by one car in front and one behind. There was nowhere to move. All of a sudden, I realized two guys were walking to the doors of my vehicle. It was like a movie scene, and I started immediately freaking out on the inside. They came to both sides of the windows, and Jay rolled his window down; the guy just started punching him in the face immediately. I quickly learned during the encounter that Jay owed this guy some money, and he was furious about it.

After he quit punching him, he told Jay that his people had surrounded him with no way to escape. He pointed out every vehicle that had us surrounded, and it was very real; we had no way of escape. He went on to tell Jay that there was a gun focused right onto his head from the car parked beside us. Jay was given very specific instructions to follow him to a secluded place, and the person with the gun would stay focused on him the entire way. If he tried anything funny, he would shoot him. Jay acted calm and said he would do everything that he was told. I was still frozen in the passenger seat, not sure what to do, and the moment the vehicles started moving, my boyfriend sped off in the other direction. I am telling you

I never in my mind would have thought that I would see something like this, much less be right in the middle of it. I did not know that things like this happened in real life. And here I was in the middle of a high-speed chase between one drug dealer and the other drug dealer because someone owed money. All of this was taking place in the middle of the city without any cops following anyone. When I would watch stuff like that happen in the movies, I would wonder where the cops were. And now here I was in a situation just like I have seen on TV, and all I could wonder was, Where are the cops? I do not know if the cops ever got called that day, but we never saw one.

Other than God having His hand in the situation, there is no other logical explanation for why no one got hurt or that there was no wreck. I cannot tell you how long the chase lasted or how far we went, but I know it went from small roads to big highways. We drove throughout the south side of Oklahoma City to Interstate 40 toward Western Oklahoma. I was not okay, and in fact, at one point, I began hyperventilating. I did not like anything I witnessed that day. The evening that I had planned for my dad's birthday did not go as intended. We still saw him, but it was hard trying to explain the black eye, and I think the visit didn't do anything but worry my dad.

I cannot remember what my mind was thinking or why I would not have drawn the line there and left him and the city, but I didn't. I knew that the people I was around and the things they were into were not good business, but since I did not physically participate in most of their activities, I somehow convinced myself that I was not guilty of anything. I was rationalizing everything so that I would not have to stop living the life I was living.

Even though I did not approve of all the things that Jay would do to make money, I stuck around because I wanted to be with someone. I wanted to be loved, so I was voluntarily blind to so much going on all around me. However, I was not completely blind to everything like him cheating on me. But I felt helpless in the situation because somehow every time I would confront him, we would fight, and it would backfire on me. I once caught him messaging another girl on my phone because he had passed out on the couch and left the phone in his hand. So I opened it and looked. Whenever I woke him up to show him I had proof, he got mad at me and broke my phone. Then he turned around and lied by telling me that his friend had used my phone the night before while I was sleeping to text a girl he liked. I did not believe him, but the story must have been convincing enough because I backed off of him, feeling like I did not have proof anymore and that I had overreacted. I then had to drive three hours back home for a new phone because mine was broken. To save money, my dad ended up giving me his phone until I could get another one.

The night that I made it back to the city with my new phone, I was exhausted because I had barely had any sleep during the last few days. I chose to go with Jay for a buy instead of staying at the apartment to sleep, and it turned out to be one of the famous waiting games. I ended up being stuck with him in the car waiting so long that I passed out. The last thing I remember was waiting outside the city for a phone call, and then I was awakened as we pulled up to my apartment so that I could go inside and sleep.

I woke up the following day on my couch, and I started looking for my phone because I was the only one home. I could not find my phone anywhere so I assumed it must be in my car. When Jay finally came home, and I looked in my car, it was nowhere to be found. When I told him that it was missing, he told me that it must have been stolen by someone with us last night, but he never did anything about it. Things like this would happen randomly throughout our relationship, but he always seemed to make up for it in a way that would make me feel like I had overreacted.

At some point, I convinced Jay to ride out to Western Oklahoma with me to meet some of my friends and old acquaintances; he finally agreed as long as he could do some business while we were there. He had a successful night and sold out practically within the first hour and with only one stop. So we had the entire night to hang out. I took Jay to my house, where my mom was staying at the time. I showed him around the house when we went into the garage, where I had a pickup parked that my dad had also bought me. It was a 1970 Chevrolet pickup that was in really good condition. My boyfriend immediately was smitten by the pickup and started asking me to take it to the city. I did not see any point in it, so I tried to brush the whole idea off; but he did not let it go that easily.

After a few hours, we ended up heading back to the city, but he continued to talk about my pickup and how much he wanted to fix it up for me and make it run even better than it already did. I was not really impressed, but his persistence began to wear me down and finally I agreed. I told my dad what I wanted to do, and he warned me that it was not a good idea and that I needed to leave the pickup right where it was. I felt led to do what pleased my dad because he was the one who bought it for me, but I could not get Jay to take no for an answer. I regretfully chose to listen to him, and we picked it up the next week and brought it to the city; it became his new obsession.

He immediately started doing what he told me he would and changing things under the hood to make it go faster and run smoother, and I have to admit it was pretty exciting and fun to watch. He became more determined to sell drugs so that he could afford to do more to the pickup. He fixed the inside, and it was nice. Not one person who rose to the challenge beat us at a stoplight in that pickup. But he was also too obsessed with it, and I started to notice that he would call it his pickup and not mine. He also started to use it to drive places without me, and I felt that he was cheating on me again. Finally, it occurred to me that the pickup needed to go back to where it belonged. I mentioned this to him, and every time I did, he would come up with just one more thing to fix or one more thing to do so it would run a little better. My dad was on me about getting it back home as well, and even though I was in the middle of stressing out about it myself, it looked to my family like I had given him a pickup that I did not. My dad even made a surprise visit to the city one day and asked where the pickup was so that he could see all that Jay had done to it. But he never got to see it because Jay told me that he had just taken the motor out of it and could not drive it to my apartment.

My dad was starting to question a lot of things at this point. I was not going to school as I had planned, and I had not gotten another job yet either. My dad had been financially supporting me, but he wondered what the point was any longer if I was not doing anything with myself or my life. Also, I could see Jay's behavior changing, and I had no clue what all he was up to. I knew that I needed to do something about it. But I had no idea where to start or how to get him to listen to me because I tried every day to get my pickup back to Western Oklahoma, but it was all without success.

IDOLATRY

Because I was trapped between my desire to use and my longing for someone to love me, the easiest thing for me to do was to "get high about it." I could so easily smoke a big blunt and not have to feel hurt, and that was my biggest fault in the relationship because I had somehow convinced myself that if I did not feel it, he was not hurting me. Now do not get me entirely wrong; I know I was pretty ignorant, but I did try to make things right. I even tried to break up with him, but he would come with greater motivation to win me back than I had a backbone. Then I would be charmed with sweet words and false promises. I tried talking with him and reasoning with him. I would tell him how he made me feel; he would apologize and show improvement, but he would soon go back to the same old ways within a matter of days. Other times I would just be accused of overreacting and being too high. I got in too far above my head, and the longer I stayed, the darker it got. The truth was that I was an all-in, fully devoted, completely sold-out meth head.

I know it is easy to see how ignorant I was and how I should have left while I was still ahead, but, likely, I am not alone on this issue. I felt it was essential to include the codependent part of my testimony because codependency and drug abuse often go hand in hand. Just as we are dependent on drugs to make us feel okay and happy, a codependent person depends on another individual to make them feel okay and satisfied. According to *Merriam-Webster* dictionary, codependency is "a psychological condition or a relationship in which a person is controlled or manipulated by another person."

The Google dictionary puts it this way: "excessive emotional or psychological reliance on a partner, typically one who requires support on account of an illness or addiction." A codependent person cannot function independently, and their thinking and behavior are organized around another person. I, my friend, was a very codependent person. I wanted to be made "whole" by how someone else made me feel. I looked to how others treated me to be okay inside. We were not made to be this way, and the truth is that according to the Bible, codependency is idolatry, and so is drug abuse.

"You shall have no other gods before Me." Exodus 20:3

Number one of the Ten Commandments that God gave Moses was having no other gods before Him. You might argue that you never looked at drugs or a person as a "god." Well, I did not think that I did either until I shed some light on this truth through the Word and heart of God. So let us start here; what is a god? According to *Merriam-Webster*, one definition of a god is a person or thing of supreme value, and another definition is "a powerful ruler." Ouch, when you put it like that, it seems that I did put other gods before the one true God. I thought of drugs and my boyfriend as having supreme value in my life. Now do not get me wrong; I know that we are to think highly of our loved ones and our significant others, but there is a fine line to be careful not to cross. If I think of anything as higher or more important than God Himself, then I have crossed the fine line and have stepped into idolatry. For me, I know that I lived for drugs, and drugs made me feel like living. I worked so that I could afford drugs, and then, on the other hand, I would only work when I was high.

When I woke up, I got high, and then I got high to fall asleep. I got high to celebrate because I was happy, and then I would get high to feel better because I was not happy. Because of drugs, I would be a faithful person, and in the same way, because of drugs, I would be an unfaithful person. Do you see how drugs were of supreme value to me? Every single part of my day involved drugs, and every aspect of my life revolved around drugs. Although it did not start that way, I quickly became a servant to drugs, and soon after, they became my god. That is idolatry. See, at first, I served the drugs faithfully, and then, as time went on, I was no longer a servant to them; I became a slave to them, and I basically bowed to their every command to get high. I promise you that if anyone had told me any of this in my active using, I would have been in complete denial and called them crazy. My mind was closed to reality, and I only saw the things that I chose to see. I depended on drugs to give me a sense of wholeness. I depended on drugs to provide me with peace, and I used them to deal with life. I depended on drugs to wake up and go to sleep. I depended on them to fulfill me, even before I sought food to fulfill me. God's word calls this idolatry because I depended on outside forces to fulfill me in ways He wants and desires to fulfill me. The truth is that we do not need anything or anyone else to give us the fulfillment that our hearts desire.

While I intoxicated my mind with drugs to give me something that I lacked, God was waiting to provide me with all I needed plus more. While I longed for someone to love me in a way that made me feel complete, God had already given that love to me through His Son. God *is* our fulfillment, and when we look toward other things to give us what only God can provide, we live our lives idolizing things of temporary pleasure and a false sense of peace. God does not run out; He is an unending supply that costs us no more than our hearts to be fully devoted to Him. God does not run away or abandon us, and I know this because His word tells us in 1 Corinthians 1:9 that He is faithful, and in Joshua 1:9, He tells us that He will be with us wherever we go. According to the word of God, He never fails to go with us, nor will He leave us; these promises are eternal because He is unchanging.

> *"Be strong and of good courage, do not fear nor be afraid*
> *of them; for the Lord your God, He is the One who goes*
> *with you. He will not leave you nor forsake you."*
> *Deuteronomy 31:6*

> *"For I am the Lord, I do not change; Therefore*
> *you are not consumed, O sons of Jacob."*
> *Malachi 3:6*

All of that is so much more than you could ever say for drugs or people because they will both run out on you, and neither one is ever a sure thing. But we can trust Him always to have what we need and when we need it. He is our sustainer and the One who helps us to endure the trials and hardships of life.

> *"Cast your burden on the Lord, And He shall sustain you;*
> *He shall never permit the righteous to be moved".*
> *Psalm 55:22*

When we put our trust in Him and give the cares of our hearts to Him, God will provide us with peace. The same peace that we have pursued through mind-altering substances is available freely through God.

> *"Be anxious for nothing, but in everything by prayer and*
> *supplication, with thanksgiving, let your requests be made known*
> *to God; and the peace of God, which surpasses all understanding,*
> *will guard your hearts and minds through Christ Jesus."*
> *Philippians 4:6-7*

God gives us joy, and our hearts can be genuinely happy without another person's influence or the use of drugs. Likewise, we can obtain a peaceful heart and mind, even in the midst of life's trials, without the use of a mind-altering substance.

> *"You will show me the path of life; In Your presence is fullness of joy; At Your right hand are pleasures forevermore."*
> Psalm 16:11

> *"Peace I leave with you, My peace I give to you; not as the world gives do I give to you. Let not your heart be troubled, neither let it be afraid".*
> John 14:27

We can be sober and sleep sweetly without using any mind-altering substances because God will even cause our sleep to be sweet.

> *"When you lie down, you will not be afraid; Yes, you will lie down, and your sleep will be sweet."*
> Proverbs 3:24

I could go on with scriptures on how God fulfills our every need, but I would end up writing the Bible if I covered them all. The Bible literally has the answers to every need in life, and if you do not believe me, check it out for yourself. I am simply giving you a taste of the things God can give us instead of seeking drugs or people to fulfill those needs.

In Matthew 6:33, it says, "But seek first the kingdom of God and His righteousness, and all these things shall be added to you." Ultimately, if we seek God first and above all else, He will be sure to take care of everything else. It is as simple as it sounds. If we can follow this simple method, then we will have everlasting peace in our hearts, knowing not only that God can take care of every single thing in our lives but also that He will.

But I did not know any of this, and although I knew of God, I did not understand that He was available to fulfill my heart and love me. I somehow got the wrong perception that God was only there to take away all the fun in my life and send my family and me to hell. I have learned differently, which is why I felt such a need to share my story. God loves us, and He is waiting to set us free from the things that have enslaved us. The word of God tells us that His people are destroyed for their lack of knowledge (Hosea 4:6), which was the case for me for so long, but His word also tells us that His mercies are new each morning (Lamentations 3:22-23). So just because I had it wrong for so long did not mean that He was not waiting for me to come to Him so that He could make all the things in my life right. I was set free from codependency toward people and drugs, and through His grace, I have been taught how to serve the one true living God, and you can learn too.

THE TRUTH ABOUT ADDICTION

The unfortunate thing about addiction is how much it blinds the people who are using it. I once took a poll with my friends on Facebook, asking them, "If you could describe addiction using only one word or phrase, what would it be?" Some of the responses I got back were "deceiving," "destructive," "blinding," "lonely," "helpless," "relentless," "sad," "sneaky," "waste," and "soul-sucking; others were "self-made prison," "killing yourself daily," "Satan's demonic hold," and "the road to ruin." From these responses, I cannot grasp why people would desire to take a chance with something that has such an evil reputation. It is literally gambling with your life.

I also gathered public responses from people who have overcome drug addiction on the reality of addiction versus the deception in the minds of those using, and this is what I gathered:

Addiction is daily lying to your family and loved ones to hide your secret.

It is putting your family and their needs on the back burner because drugs are more important.

Addiction is pushing away every person in your life who cares because they "do not understand."

It is building walls and burning bridges between every relationship you have.

Addiction is feeling guilty because you wasted your entire day searching for a fix, so you promise yourself, "Tomorrow I will do better."

It is repeating that cycle the moment you run out because the high controls your life.

Addiction is compromising everything about yourself and throwing away every moral that you have ever had just for a high.

It is waking up the next day and doing it again despite how ashamed you are of the night before.

Addiction is lying to your spouse and children.

It is trading your family for a high.

Addiction is leaving your children at someone else's home for a week at a time.

It is not seeing your babies grow up.

Addiction is using your paycheck to re-up even if the rent or electricity is due.

It is making sure you get high even if it means going without food.

Addiction is losing the trust of every person who knows you.

It is being at family events and not being able to go to the bathroom without someone watching your every move so that you won't steal their things.

Addiction is heartbreaking to all those who love and care about you.

It is putting them through sleepless nights and worry-filled days.

Addiction is trying so desperately to numb yourself and escape all of the heartaches.

It is actually creating more heartaches.

Addiction is choosing to live in chains of shame, defeat, and misery.

It is being blinded to the reality that you are putting yourself deeper into the pit every time you pick up the pipe, roll the joint, or swallow the pill.

Addiction is where Satan wants you because drugs are the tools he uses to slowly kill you spiritually and physically.

It is never wanting to stop because you have become so dead inside that only the high can make you feel alive.

To those who have never used before, all of this may seem like a no-brainer; one may not understand why a person would choose that life, but as I said, it is very deceptive. While using drugs, the truth is not obvious; I am not making excuses for myself or anyone because, ultimately, it is still the individual's choice to make. But I will say that I never once understood any of this when I was actively using because my eyes were blind to reality. I knew the reality of my life, but somehow, I felt like it was always the people around me with the problem and not me. I was living with a boyfriend who treated me worse than anyone had ever treated me in my life, but I stayed. In my addiction to the drugs he sold and my codependent mindset I had no strength or ability to walk away. I was being used so badly, but I somehow convinced myself I was not and that he really did love me or he would not still be with me. I did not listen to family or friends if they tried to tell me any different, so of course, I isolated myself away from all the people who genuinely cared about me because they kept trying to tell me the truth. So while isolating myself, I started to lose control of my life more and more.

STOLEN AND ARRESTED

I had reached a place in my life where I was taking one step forward and two steps back. I was in the midst of a fast-paced life, drug dealing, never slowing down and doing anything but hustle after another high, and I was missing the good old days when I got high to have a good time and not as a way of survival. I was getting worn down mentally, and the drugs were not reviving me anymore as they once had. They just seemed to pull me deeper and deeper into a pit instead. I was in a battle for my soul, and with each passing day, my will to live was becoming less and less.

This reality hit me hard the night I laid in the passenger seat of my car. My boyfriend was using me for all that I had and controlled every part of my day. I never liked being part of selling drugs to begin with, yet I was being forced to tag along—even to the point of him making me sit in my car while he went into a dealer's house to cheat on me. When I broke, I broke entirely before God that night, and even though I did not truly realize it, God started working on my life right then and there.

I did not intentionally forget to tell my boyfriend that I called my dad to come and get me that night because when Jay got back in the car, he gave me some undeniable excuse and pretended like everything in our world was perfectly fine. I think he subconsciously felt bad when he would do me wrong because he would work extra hard for a few days to treat me like gold to compensate for his actions. It would seem like when I gained the strength to leave him, he would turn around and be the best boyfriend I ever had. I was waiting for the right moment to tell him that I was leaving him, and I had completely lost track of time.

When my sister called me that day, we had just met up with a potential new dealer in the middle of the parking lot of a shopping center. It was someone Jay had just connected with the night before, and the guy wanted to get to know him better before he dealt with him. We had just pulled up next to each other to talk when I answered my phone. I hung up after the call and looked at Jay, and I told him that we needed to talk ASAP because I had my family at my apartment ready to move my things. We had all of our drugs and paraphernalia put in a safe in the apartment; they did not have a key to get in, but he knew how fast we needed to get there before the wrong person showed up while we were not there. Jay told the new guy we had an emergency and would have to meet up with him later. He drove off, asking me what was going on. I told him about the night that he was in the dealer's house with the girl and how I called my dad wanting to go home. I explained how I struggled to find the right time to tell him about it and how things between us throughout the week were going so well that I had completely forgotten all about it. Then in the middle of me explaining to him, the words that I would never have expected came out of his mouth, "I want to go with you and get out of this life." Jay continued to tell me that he was getting tired of living the drug-dealer life, and he wanted to settle down with me and stop doing what he was doing so that he could stay out of prison.

You see, he had already been in jail quite a few times and had a hefty record. I had no clue about the extent of his crimes or any knowledge that he was facing prison at this time, but I will get into that later on. I was just in complete shock and yet on cloud nine at the same time. I just knew in my heart this was going to be the big break I had been hoping for and that he would move to a small town and stop selling and get a job. My heart began to hope for the first time in a while.

When I got to my apartment, I told my family about the new plan and how Jay was coming back with me and that I needed at least one more week so he could take care of things and go with me. They were not backing down on getting me home, but I convinced them that if they would take all of the big stuff and leave some basic things behind, I could stay another week and then bring the rest of my things in the car. My dad seemed slightly satisfied that day to see that my pickup was still physically there, but he was more concerned with getting me home and away from there.

I can't tell you that my life immediately got better and that God fixed everything that I had messed up in my life. I can't tell you this for one reason: I was unwilling to let go of the drugs. I begged God to help me, but I was unwilling to let go of the only thing that was dragging me down. Drugs. I wanted God to fix all of the messed-up stuff in my life but then leave me free to do the things I wanted. I still wanted to live life the way I wanted and how I wanted to on my terms.

While I was working to get things together to move, Jay was busy taking care of business. He was trying to walk out cleanhanded, and to this day, I do not know the real story or the actual business he had to handle. I only knew that he owed a few people money. So while he was extra busy on the streets, I was actually at my apartment cleaning and getting the rest of the things ready to move. And while I was excited and hopeful about my future, I had no clue what lay before me. Jay had been staying out extra-long hours and doing extra deals, all while working to put back together the motor that he had taken out of the pickup, again.

One day I had been out with him, but I had already been up too long and told him that I needed to get to the apartment so that I could get some sleep. So he dropped me off and said that he had a few other things to take care of but that he would be shortly behind me. So I went to the apartment and went to sleep. Then I remember him showing up sometime in the middle of the night, but I just went back to sleep when he crawled into bed. It seemed like it was hardly ever just the two of us because he always had someone who worked by his side. So it was not uncommon to have a third wheel in the apartment, either hanging out in the living room or asleep on the couch.

I do not know how much time had passed, but the next thing I remember is his buddy banging on the bedroom door, saying, "Someone just drove off with your truck!" I woke up confused because that did not even make sense to me. So I woke Jay up to tell him to go and look outside, and he came crawling back into bed saying, yes, someone had stolen the truck. Because he didn't seem all that worried about it, and I was exhausted, I just went right back to sleep, not believing what I had heard.

I think we slept another twenty-four hours at least. When I had enough strength, I got up and looked outside my apartment window, and, sure enough, my car was there but not my pickup. I woke up Jay freaking out about the whole deal, but my boyfriend was not nearly as upset about it as I was; he was mad, it seemed, yet calm like it was something that happens all the time. He said that I just needed to call the cops and report it as stolen. I felt like he should be the one doing the reporting because I had no clue what was going on, but he always had some warrant out for him and, therefore, could not deal with cops.

So I called the cops, and a police officer met me outside my apartment to file a report. Dealing with police officers was entirely new territory for me. I had no clue what I was doing, and because cops ask all sorts of questions about who was where and what time it was when it happened, I had to lie about everything except that my pickup had been stolen. But it was hard for me to truthfully answer any of these questions because I had not even been with my pickup these past few days. I genuinely cared for the whereabouts of my vehicle, and all the while, Jay just sat up in the apartment getting high with his buddy while I was taking care of his dirty work. When I finished talking with the police officer and went back up to the apartment, my boyfriend started telling me of all the people who could have possibly stolen it and that he would work harder than the cops to find it. I then had to make one of the most challenging phone calls I have ever had to make. I had to call my dad and tell him what happened, and he immediately accused Jay and me of selling it. I do not blame my dad for accusing me, but it hurt that he did not believe me. But, of course, I was blinded by the real truth of the events, and I believed Jay when he said he had no idea or involvement in it whatsoever. In light of everything, I felt like I did not belong to this kind of life, and I was ready to get back to Western Oklahoma and start something different, but Jay had other plans. He wanted to find out who stole the pickup.

So our week of packing turned into two weeks, and in those two weeks, he became obsessed with finding the truck and the person who stole it. I was kind of in tune with that idea the first week, but after driving around the entire Oklahoma City area, day and night, up and down every street, it started to get old and depressing to me; I just wanted to leave it behind. I was not sure why he felt the need to find it. Maybe it was because it genuinely made it look like he had nothing to do with it. But as I look back now, it just makes him look even more guilty, like he had to put on a massive show to prove himself to me. So I stopped riding with him and went back to packing my things and cleaning the apartment because there were only a few days left to get everything cleaned and moved.

While Jay was on this adventure to look for the pickup, he got involved quite heavily with a local gang to help him find it. I was completely uncomfortable with the whole deal, and I would hardly allow myself to be around any of them. Even though I had gotten the apartment cleaned and taken care of, I would still go there and sit in the empty rooms because I did not want to be around all of the crazy stuff he was doing while looking for the pickup. I was uncomfortable and unhappy, and I wanted to leave. I was just waiting on him to give it up.

Then one morning, he came to the apartment and told me that he was pretty sure he knew where the truck was and that I needed to load up and go with him. So he drove us to this random house in the Midwest City area, and sure enough, there was my truck in the backyard, completely stripped out and nothing but a frame and parts of the colors showing that it had been my pickup. He jumped out of the car and ran to it while I followed, and I was just so heartbroken. When he talked about finding my pickup, I was just so sure he meant like find it as a whole. I never even imagined it would be just a frame. Despite what was left of the pickup, he assured me that I needed to call 911 and inform them that I had found my stolen pickup, and while I was on the phone with 911, he left, telling me that he could not be here when the cops showed up. So there I was, all alone, waiting for the cops to come and rescue my pickup and hopefully make things all right and arrest the person in the house. But that is not what happened.

Apparently, to everyone but me, it was a drug deal gone bad. The cops had just arrested the person who lived in this house the previous week for something else, and they already knew where my pickup was. They were just waiting for it to all fall into place for their benefit, and I guess it did. Somehow, they got wind of Jay's name, and they were just baiting him and me apparently. I ended up getting arrested that day because they searched me and found a meth pipe in my purse. Some cops found Jay down the road watching the whole thing; he was arrested because of his outstanding warrant. We were taken to different county jails; I was taken to Cleveland County jail. He was taken to Oklahoma County jail because of his warrant from Oklahoma County.

When I was being booked in the jail, I was allowed my one phone call, and I called my dad's friend who lived in the city. I do not know why I did that, but I was in shock over the whole thing. I was afraid I would not be given a second call if I called my dad and he did not answer because he was out in the field working. So I told the family friend what happened, and I told him where I was and that I needed him to please call and tell my dad. Then I was led to my cell, and I remember hearing whistles and men yelling as I was being taken to my cell. I was the only one in the cell I was put in, and I just laid down and slept. I remember them giving me food, but I was too tired to eat.

The next thing I knew, my dad was bonding me out and my sister Kristel was with him. I cannot remember the events after that, where I went or how long my boyfriend stayed in Oklahoma County jail. All I remember of that arrest was when I had to make the phone call and ask my dad's friend to tell my dad what had happened because it broke my heart even more than losing the pickup. I know it looked like I was in on the whole pickup thing, but I had no clue how badly I was being played and manipulated. Honestly, as I write this, I think to myself, "Jennie! How dumb were you?!" But if sharing my mistakes with someone else will help them overcome what they are going through, I am glad to share it.

FAILED ATTEMPTS TO CHANGE

My family finally realized what had been going on with me and my life. I was on drugs, and so was my boyfriend. My family was disappointed, but they loved me and wanted me to get right. Technically I was a big girl, so even though they knew this was a bad idea, they could not make life decisions for me. So I chose to believe that my boyfriend was innocent, and I stayed with him. After we were both bailed out of jail the following week, we finally moved to Western Oklahoma, and we did play it low-key for a while. We never stayed sober, but we did calm down a lot. And even though he was inevitably facing prison time, I felt like things were looking up because we were no longer in the city dealing drugs.

I started working again at the same steakhouse I worked at when I was in high school, and I could see my family more. My boyfriend was working on vehicles around town. We did not do the best we could have because we spent so much of our money on drugs, but we felt good about it because it was earned money. For a time, my heart was happier; he stayed away from most people from the city, which made our relationship grow like never before. I told my family I was sober just because I felt I could do a better job hiding it this time and that I could live life like everyone else lived theirs and yet stay high. Well, spoiler alert—that is not how it worked or ever will work.

We both eventually decided that we wanted to go back to the city and see some old friends for a fun night. That was a bad idea because it just fanned an old flame, and Jay was quickly convinced that he would just buy some drugs with his earned money to sell a little in

Western Oklahoma so that we could get high without it costing us out of pocket. It was not something I thought was a good idea, but it sounded convincing enough for me to go for it. So just like that, he was back to the hustle, and I was back to following him around as he did it. It eventually became the biggest priority in our lives again and interfered with my actual job, so I just quit it and went back full time to the life that I just tried to escape. It did not take long before I was just as miserable doing it as I was before. This time, the only difference was that we had to drive back and forth on the interstate, and we were constantly in the car and never home.

It was the same cycle. We were back to fighting and back to jealousy and back to insanity, and in the midst of the insanity, my car got wrecked and totaled; only by the grace of God were our lives spared. One night I was beyond tired and needed some sleep, and I did not even feel like trying to fight it—I just wanted to sleep. Not only was it because I was past my three-day mark but after you are up for so long, you do not even feel high when you are using; it's like you are just using to keep your mind and body from crashing. It is so unhealthy. I just liked the feeling of feeling high, so whenever I got to that point, I was always willing to lie down and sleep. Jay wanted to go back to the city, though, and he told me that if I did not go with him, he was taking my car without me. I did not trust him to go by himself for so many reasons: first, he didn't even have a license; second, I felt he was to blame for losing the truck that my dad had given me; and third, I just had a gut feeling that it was not a good idea. I tried to convince him that we should stay home and sleep for a little while and then go, but he would not listen to me. So I felt I had no choice but just to shut up and get in the car. I do not even remember making it out of town that night before I fell asleep.

The next thing that I remember is feeling my car jerk hard to one side and then back to the other side and then Jay pulling over, stopping the car, and telling me to grab my stuff and get out. I had no idea what had happened, but I quickly did as he said because he sounded serious and urgent. At that time, I had a brown Labrador Retriever puppy named Busa, who went everywhere with me. Busa was in the car with us, so I grabbed him and my purse and followed Jay up the hill to the overpass. We had just left my car off the side of the interstate, and I had no clue what had happened. He kept telling me that my car had messed up and that it caused him to almost crash and that we had to get away from the scene because we had weed on us and he had a warrant out for his arrest.

So we walked a mile away from the interstate and then for miles and miles more toward the city until he finally got ahold of someone to come and pick us up. I cannot remember the exact time. All I know is that the sun was coming up by the time we got in a vehicle. I was upset the whole time because I knew I would upset my family again, and I had no clue what had just happened. Finally, we made it to the drug dealer's house, and we got high and hung out awhile, trying to figure out what to do. Then I got a phone call from a highway patrolman. He told me that my car was found off the side of the interstate and if I wanted to know where it was impounded, I needed to meet him at a specific place at a specific time. I was so upset. I did not like any of this kind of stuff. I wanted to get high, but I never was into doing things that were against the rules. Because of his warrant, Jay told me that I had to go by myself, and he gave me some story about how the tie-rod in the car broke and caused me to crash and that I called a family member to pick me up. My boyfriend called his aunt and had her take me to meet the highway patrolman. As soon as I arrived, the officer told me what had happened based on the evidence, and I did not have any room to argue with him. I assumed he did not even want to take the time to listen to my side of the story, knowing it would just be a lie anyway.

He fined me for reckless driving and for leaving the scene of an accident. Then he started to question who I was with and why. I thought that he would go further and find a reason to arrest me, but he ended up letting me go. I called Jay furious over the whole ordeal, and he barely seemed to care that I had just caught him lying to me. He had fallen asleep while driving and wrecked my car—and I got fined for it. When his aunt and I got back from talking to the officer, I could not find him anywhere at the drug dealer's house. Jay's mom was there, so I asked her where he was, and she acted like she didn't know; but I could tell that she just did not want to tell me anything. It was always really twisted how his mom and sister would cover for him and his weird shenanigans. I just went outside to the little garage that had been turned into an apartment, and the moment I got to the door, he and a girl we knew opened the door. I am sure that just by telling you this, how obvious it is as to what they were doing, but he just played it cool. When I asked him what they were doing, he said, "nothing." I did not push too hard at the moment because I did not feel like fighting at the drug dealer's house. Plus, I had a bigger issue—I had to call my dad and tell him about my car and that I needed a ride home.

    I called him, and of course, he was not happy. My dad has always been such a caring dad and has always loved me, but he is frank in sharing his opinions and feelings; I knew that he would unleash on me and he had every reason to. So after talking with him and sounding like a complete idiot about what had happened, I got it arranged for him to come and pick us up in the city, and by then, we needed to leave the dealer's house anyways. So we went over to Jay's mom's house and waited. We were not at her house for ten minutes before he passed out, and when he passed out, there was no waking him up. I just hoped that he would get enough sleep in the three hours it would take for my dad to drive there so he could wake up when he got there. As the time got closer, I tried everything that I could think of to wake him up, and up until the very moment when my dad was outside in the driveway, he stayed passed out. Everything we did was suspicious at this point in our lives, but my family did not have proof that we were still on drugs. So it was really important to hide all of the sketchy stuff, like being passed out without being able to be woken up.

My dad drove us home, and then two days later, we got a call from the insurance agency saying that my car was going to be totaled. When Jay had fallen asleep behind the wheel, he veered to the left and hit a guardrail and then somehow bounced back over on top of the other guardrail and straddled it, pulling out all of the stuff underneath my car. It is such a miracle that neither of us was hurt or anyone else. So just like that, my car was totaled, and now I was without a vehicle.

Looking back, I can still see how God had different plans for me all along, and those plans seemed to have been ignited the night that I cried out to Him for help. Everything that went wrong in the moment seemed like something in life hated me, like no matter what I did or what direction I went, it would get messed up. But now that I am clearheaded and God-conscious, I see how God knew the trouble that lay ahead of me. Even though I had not pursued Him since the night I cried out to Him in my car, He never forgot my cry for help. He never left my side because He knew that I still did not have it in me to get better without Him, so He was just there gently closing doors for me to protect me and get me to go in a different direction.

God does not force us to do His will, so even though His mercy will save us time and time again, He will not make us do anything. He has given us a free will to choose. Like you and I, we do not force anyone to love us because it would not be true love. God waits for us to be ready to come to Him because He will not force us.

After a couple of months and with the help of my dad, I finally got another vehicle. For the time being, not having a vehicle was a good thing because we did not have any way to drive to the city, and it kept us at home. But eventually, the cycle just started all over again. Whenever we did go, we just had intentions to drive back up there to re-up, but that is not what happened because once we went up there and got more, the cycle started back all over again. So it did not take very long before we got arrested again.

The day we got arrested again, we were in Oklahoma City, and it was a crazy day. First, we kept running into people we had not seen since before our first arrest, and it kept giving me an uneasy feeling, like to the pit of my stomach. I kept telling Jay, "I do not have a good feeling about today; I think we need to go home and forget the buy." He'd say, "We'll just get some and then go." But we could not find anything with our normal people; everyone everywhere was out. Then, while we were waiting, he said he needed to visit his baby momma to talk about their son.

I always went in with him, but this time he told me I had to wait outside because he needed to talk to her alone because he wanted to convince her to let his son come and live with us. I did not like the idea of him going in alone, but he made it sound convincing enough. So I sat out in that pickup, waiting for him, for I do not even know how long. I would text him and get no reply. I had a gut feeling about what he was up to, but I did not have it in me to do anything about it. I finally broke down and called my sister Kristel. She was always close to my dad and helped him out a lot, especially when I was gone and living a hectic life. I just broke down over the phone and explained the situation to her. I told her that I had my pickup, but he took all the money; I had no way to go anywhere because I hardly had any fuel. She calmed me down and told me that she would have my dad transfer just enough money into my bank account to use my debit card for gas and come home.

I just remember feeling so heartbroken because I thought that driving away meant giving up on all the progress I thought we had made. I wanted to keep working at fixing something and someone who did not wish to be fixed, but I did not yet have the wisdom to know that you cannot change people who do not want to be changed. About ten minutes after I called my sister, I drove off, put some gas in my truck, and headed back on I-40 toward Western Oklahoma.

I was almost halfway home when Jay texted me as if nothing was wrong, saying, "I think I found where we can get some." I wanted to ignore the message, but then my heart convinced me that I was overreacting and should have never left. So I turned around at the next exit and headed back to the city as quickly as possible. Once I arrived, he came out shortly after I pulled into the parking lot and asked me why I had left, so I told him the truth. His only response was to ask me how much money they transferred to me. I told him that I did not want to use it for drugs because I genuinely felt bad about the entire situation. He convinced me that if I could get to an ATM and withdraw the cash, we could buy more than we already had planned, and he would make money back for me to put back into my account, just like we had never used it. I was hesitant, but I went for it. I told him that we needed to buy and return home because I still had a gut feeling something bad was fixing to happen. He would not take me seriously and just told me I was paranoid.

We finally made it to the house where we were told we would be able to buy what we wanted. This was one of those so-and-so knows so-and-so kind of deals. We did not know these people, and we had never been to this side of town. I was nearly having a panic attack on the inside because when we walked into the house, I could immediately tell that some sketchy stuff went on around this place. There was not one piece of furniture in this house—no kitchen table and not one chair; it was empty of furniture but full of people. There were people off in every room doing something. I tried my best not to look at anyone or what they were doing. I remember walking through the kitchen where a group of girls were standing talking to a guy as we were led into the farthest bedroom to speak to the guy who had the drugs so that we could do the deal.

I knew in this situation not to say a word to anyone unless I was spoken to first. Even my naive mind knew I was in a house run by a pimp, full of prostitutes. When we walked into another furnitureless room, we saw the dealer, standing there without a shirt on, plainly revealing his big, shiny pistol. I just remember looking toward the ground. I did not want to see his face, and I did not want to look at his gun. I just wanted to run out of there so bad for many reasons, not to mention that we were literally the only white people in the house. I promise you I am not the least racist, and I have had dealings with many people of different colors, but we were entirely out of our element that day. Fortunately, the exchange happened rather quickly, and the moment we were out of there and into the pickup, it was such a sigh of relief. I told Jay that was scary and that I never wanted to go there again, and he agreed with me.

We started to head back to the south side of the city to pick up Busa from Jay's mom's house and get high there before driving back west. As we started, we saw a girl we knew talking to two guys, so we pulled into the parking lot to see what she was doing because we had not seen her in a while. When the two guys turned around, they immediately asked my boyfriend for his driver's license, which he did not have. It turns out that they were undercover cops, and it escalated from there. They found his drugs and handcuffed us both. They ended up handcuffing the girl they were talking to, but I have no clue what she even did. I knew that my dad and family would be so disappointed in me. I just could not get things right in life.

We got put in the police car, and the police officer drove us to another part of town. We pulled into a McDonald's parking lot, and the officer opened the door. When I stepped out, the two undercover cops who initially arrested us were standing there, separately giving each of us a chance to be a part of some kind of controlled buys so that we could possibly lessen our sentence. I wanted no part of any of it because I knew how dangerous that was. When we arrived in the Oklahoma Country jail, it was nothing like I had experienced yet. So many people had gotten arrested that I could not even count them. Jay and I got separated because I had to go and sit with the women. I am not sure how long it took to get booked, but I think it was several hours. The jailers who booked us were all hateful, and they made fun of everyone as we were getting our mug shots taken.

I was sitting off in the far corner, as secluded as I could be, when a lady came over to me and asked if she could sit in my spot. I kindly declined. She replied sternly, "I need to sit in your spot."

Soon the girl who got arrested with us said, "Jennie, you need to let her sit there."

So I just listened and moved over, and it was not long before I realized why. The girl had meth on her, and she was disposing of it all by eating it. I could literally hear her crunching on huge rocks of meth as quickly as she could to dispose of them. I was afraid that she would overdose, but I knew not to say anything; I had to sit there like I had not witnessed a thing.

The girl I knew and I got separated when we were assigned to our cells. I walked into a cell with another girl already in there; we introduced ourselves, and I quickly laid down and went to sleep. The next day as I talked to my cellmate, I learned that she did not have a drug problem like most of the people there—she just had an anger problem. She was a lesbian who had been arrested for trying to run over her girlfriend, who had just broken up with her. Given that this girl was quite a bit bigger than me, I was in a strange predicament. She was friendly to me, but I stood my ground with her when necessary and sternly set boundaries. I do not know how tough I looked, but I tried to be bold with her. To be honest, I was not sure what was going to happen.

My dad chose not to bail me out as quickly this time and let me stay there a week, and it was rough. I do not wish that place on anyone. My small-town mentality had no clue of the real racial differences in a place like that. I figured that out quickly on the day that I sat at a table full of Hispanics. I guess moments like that made having a bigger girl for a cellmate come in handy.

I was so grateful and relieved the day my dad finally bailed me out. But my happiness was quick to disappear once I found out Jay had been bailed out after only two days, and he never even tried to bail me out. Instead, he lied and told me he thought I had already been bailed out and was not answering his phone calls. I went home alone that night, pretty distraught about the whole thing. I felt used in so many ways, but I did not know what to do about it. I was hurting my family, and I knew it but did not know how to stop. I spent a few days sober at my dad's, wallowing in my despair and confusion. Then Jay called and said he wanted to come back to Western Oklahoma. For some reason, I felt like things might be hopeful again, but that was not the reality. Things never got better for us no matter how hard we tried.

Every turn I made, it seemed like life was against me and kept shutting me down no matter how hard I tried to be careful. Have you ever watched *Final Destination* in which people somehow escape their fate of death in a moment's time, and then it was as if fate was mad about it and death was coming to them in the most bizarre accidents and incidents? In a manner of speaking, that is what my life had become. It did not matter what direction I took or what decision I made, each and every step led me to jail or a dead end. I will not say that I was innocent in all of the situations because I was just as guilty for being there and being high, but I will say to this day that every charge I ever got outside of a possession charge was not what I was doing. Because of this, I felt like life was against me, people were against me, and basically that the world was against me. I blamed the cops for profiling me. I blamed people for snitching on the wrong people. I blamed fate. I blamed everything except God. I would have blamed Him; I am sure if I had acknowledged His existence. It seemed that after He answered me once, I completely forgot who He was again.

I believe wholeheartedly today that God was trying to shut me down and get me out of the drug life every time I got arrested. I know it is not a way that anyone would want God to use to get their attention, but it will definitely stop a person long enough to give them a chance to hear Him. But I still was not trying to look His way, so it took me a while to catch on to what God was doing. After we got arrested that time, my boyfriend was sure to have prison time very soon, so it just seemed like we were just staying together on borrowed time. I was fortunate to have had all cases dismissed or gotten probation, but that would not last forever either as it will always eventually catch up.

I know that reading everything I have written makes it obvious how badly my boyfriend was using me. I am aware of how smart it makes me look for staying with him as well. But I must say that I know he loved me. He was just not mentally healthy, and neither was I. I had endured rejection growing up and felt it enough with my previous boyfriend that my self-esteem was at its lowest. I did not know about self-worth, and when you do not love and respect yourself, you do not love and respect anyone else. Jay and I did have some really good days, and we obviously had some really bad ones; it was so easy just to get high and forget the bad ones. I felt in my heart that I could somehow save him from the lifestyle of a drug dealer and show him a better way to live life because I knew that his upbringing was not perfect. But what it comes down to is no one can change anyone, no matter how much they love each other. The person who needs change can only be changed when they desire it.

There also comes a time in broken relationships like this when people need to just walk away from each other because it is that unhealthy. He knew he would be going to prison soon, so it was like he stopped caring about trying to get right. He started doing things I had never seen him do before. I kept fighting him on it, and it just got really bad. I was getting mentally exhausted fighting my own demons, plus the fact that I was trying to heal him of his demons at the same time. I rode around in my car for one week in the city with barely any sleep in one instance. I was exhausted physically and mentally. I had to get really high one night just to make the drive back because we were hours away from Western Oklahoma. I remember thinking I had never had so much go wrong in my life. I kept thinking how badly I just wanted to be okay. I did not feel like the drugs gave me the satisfaction they always had before, and I could not get numb enough. When we finally made it home, I immediately tried to go to sleep, but my mind would not rest. I got frustrated; I did not have any weed to counteract the meth, so I checked in the medicine cabinet and found some Benadryl and just felt compelled to take a bunch of pills.

I do not remember thinking that I wanted to die or harm myself. I just wanted to sleep, and I wanted to be numb. I cannot even tell you how many I took, but I immediately realized that I had messed up and started trying to make myself throw up. When Jay realized what I had just done, he called my mom, and she was there immediately. I cried for her not to take me to the hospital because I thought it would be okay if I just kept trying to make myself throw up, but she knew better and made me go. Once I got to the hospital, the drowsiness started to really kick in, and I remember them making me eat this really nasty charcoal paste; then I got so tired I could not keep my eyes open anymore. I fell asleep as the doctor was talking to me.

I was admitted to the local hospital, and I was being observed for a few days. I hardly remember anything while I was there. I remember opening my eyes and seeing my mom every time, and I remember seeing two friends of mine crying at the foot of my bed. I remember hearing my dad's voice once, and I remember seeing my eldest sister Tisha once; and that is all. I know now without a doubt that God spared my life once again. I slept for days, and when I was stable and could stay awake, I was transferred to a state facility for a mental evaluation.

SOBRIETY OR PRISON

On the other side of the chaos, my boyfriend got arrested in my hometown for some other reason, so he was locked up. A mind with common sense would say, "This is enough!" but I could not see it that way because I was still blinded. The night that I had overdosed should have been my rock bottom, but it was not. The day my dad and sister picked me up from the mental institution should have been my rock bottom, but it was not. I remember them picking me up and agreeing with my dad that I needed to go and stay with him for a time. We went to my house to grab my clothes, and I immediately grabbed my stash of meth and then went to my dad's house to "get better." I planned to stay with him for a while and get my life back on track. I guess a part of me felt now that my family knew all of my big secrets that kept me so far away from them, I could start over with a fresh plate of using behind their backs as I did from the beginning.

I told myself that I would work harder to do better in life by getting a job and taking care of myself, but I never intended to stop getting high. I had a mile-long mental list of things not to do next time or people never to trust again so that I could "learn" from my mistakes, but the list did not include sobriety. Jay was so close to serving prison time, and by now, the years were stacking. Of course, I promised to wait on him, and I had honest intentions too. A month or so later, he was sentenced and transferred to prison; we promised each other that we would stay sober because we both knew that sobriety was the best choice. We were both happier that way, but that promise was easier said than done.

My sobriety lasted a week and a few days, and then I started getting high again. The only difference was that I could do it all with more freedom, or so to speak, because this time, I had more control in our relationship than I had ever had. I was able to go and do more things than I had been able to do in a long time. I could be around my friends because I did not have to put on a front like I was happy when I was miserable. I had a job; it appeared like I was doing better on the outside, and as far as my family knew, I was.

And then I got arrested again—another bizarre charge that seemed as if fate was just trapping me. At this point in my life, I was at the end of my rope as far as the justice system went; they were tired of messing with me. The court offered me prison time or a program called Drug Court, and I thought my life was over as I knew it because I had no clue how to even try to stay sober. But you know how sentencing can sometimes take months to come to completion, so there I was, running wide open convinced I did not have a drug problem but instead that the world had a problem with me.

I remember reading this poem called "I Am Crystal Meth" as a kid when I knew that my mom was on drugs, and when I read it now, it still passes my understanding of how deceitful and evil this drug is. Every single part of this poem is 100 percent accurate. I think the most deceitful part about meth is that the user believes they are in control of it when it is in control of them. I do not believe that is just toward meth. I think that goes for all mind-altering substances. That poem can sum up my entire story and many others' as well. All that meth and drugs were for me and are for thousands of others is a tool that Satan uses to ruin lives. The weed: a tool. The pills: a tool. The alcohol: a tool. All mind-altering substances are tools of the enemy who desires nothing for your life but to kill, steal, and destroy it (John 10:10).

Many people have tried to run from addiction as I have, but it is impossible to run from a problem you are constantly pouring into your own soul. Changing your people, places, and things is a good and necessary thing to do, but without trying to make changes to your mind and heart, it is just like a bear going into hibernation. Just because the bear is not eating or walking around looking for food for a season does not mean that he will not eventually because it is just a matter of time. When that time comes and he wakes up, he will be hungry, violently searching for some food. I would try to stay sober, but the moment I was around someone else who used, it was like my inner bear awoke. It could be a complete stranger I had never known before, and somehow within ten minutes of conversation, we would have figured out that we both liked the same kind of drug. Whether it was weed, pills, or meth. As I said, you cannot run from a problem that is within yourself.

I continued to write Jay letters every night and talked to him like I was staying sober and faithful to him. But really, I was not even trying to do right for him because my addiction had reached a whole new level. My mom and I had a falling out due to our drug use because that is just what drugs do—they tear you and everyone around you apart. I felt like everyone was against anything I wanted to do in my life. So my mom and I stopped talking, and the rest of my family had no idea what to think of me anymore.

In the same way, my eldest sister had completely stopped all contact with me because she could not handle watching me ruin my life anymore. However, my dad and other sister still dealt with me and all of my stuff on a constant basis. When all of this would happen, I felt like they were stressing themselves out by worrying about things they needed to stay out of because I thought my drug abuse did not hurt anyone but myself. Well, that is wrong, wrong, wrong. I was hurting everyone around me.

The time finally came for my final court date, and on the day of the final sentencing, my mom showed up at my house with Kristel and my dad. I was angry she was there, but she was calm and tried to be peaceful toward me. She came into my room as I was getting ready to go to court and told me that she had been sober for the last couple of months, but I did not believe her. I felt that she was just putting up a front to win over my dad and sister somehow. My family and I all got into the same vehicle and drove to court. I walked into court that day facing multiple years for a crime I was not a part of, but I had no more room to fight the system. It would not have mattered if I had fought them on the bogus charge because I was already on probation and should not have been associating with the person involved. I was offered a trial, which would have led to more prison time if I was counted guilty, or I could take Drug Court. As a desperate attempt to just stay out of prison, I chose Drug Court. I had no desire for the program whatsoever, but I had even less desire for prison time. I did not know how I was going to do it, but I wanted to do the program correctly because I was terrified of the idea of prison. I had full intentions to go back to living my life the way that I wanted once I completed the program.

Drug Court is a program that is an alternative to incarceration. It provides offenders an opportunity to receive treatment and education about addiction while teaching them how to live a life without the use of drugs. Drug Court participants live in the real world like everyone else, but they are under strict supervision. They must abstain from substance abuse and alcohol for the duration of the program to learn to be functioning adults in an everyday functioning world because many addicts have either forgotten how to or were never taught how. As many addicts have lived the life of hustling and unaccountability for so long, any other way of life becomes foreign to them. To be honest, this program sounded horrendous to me—but just a little better than prison. I was so afraid and had no idea how I was going to be sober or stay sober. I had all of these fearful anxiety attacks come over me, like, "How am I going to ever deal with myself if someone I love dies?" "How do I find the energy to go to work when I am so exhausted?" "What if I fail and go to prison and I have no one?" But my sister Kristel kept trying to reassure me that I could do it and promised me that it would be okay and that she was right by my side through it all. But even with her best attempt to encourage me, I felt hopeless.

As they dropped me off at my house after court, my mom came inside with me, and she continued trying to tell me that everything would be okay. She also continued to tell me how she had found God and that He had given her a new life and freedom from drugs. I was so mad. I did not want to hear anything she had to say because it sounded crazy. Then she offered to take me to all the things I had to go do to get set up in Drug Court. I was okay with that offer just because my mind was so clouded, and it was hard to stay focused, much less do any of it and stay awake while doing it. I had intakes, assessments, meetings, and court to attend in one week.

My family left, and I had to go through my house and flush the weed I wanted so badly to just smoke. I gathered all of my paraphernalia and put it into a box, and about that same time, I heard a knock on my door. I opened it to see that a friend of mine had come over to get high with me. I was not sure what to do with my box of paraphernalia up until that moment, so I just grabbed the box and gave it to him and told him to come back in two years and get me high because I was now in Drug Court. He left happy that day, but me not so much; I had to go lie down and sleep the rest of the day.

Throughout that week, my mom and dad drove me to all of my appointments and the places I had to go to for Drug Court. All I could do was sleep. I would lie down in the car as my parents drove me to places, and I would wake up for my appointments. That first week was a real fog. I just remember sleeping and eating. Looking back, I probably needed some kind of detox time because those days were really brutal, and I can hardly remember any of it. The court told me that I needed to start attending twelve-step meetings, and it had to be ninety meetings in ninety days. But I did not understand that they literally meant start it right now; I just assumed it was to be started at some point. My mom kept being so helpful and caring that I could not stay mad at her, but I still did not think she was sober. I kept thinking in the back of my mind that she must be up to something.

My first Drug Court appearance was on a Monday, exactly one week after I had signed for it. I felt like it took all the strength I had in me to get dressed and put makeup on that day. When I showed up, and my name got called, they asked to see the progress of my meetings, which I had not started yet. They also asked why I failed my drug test for meth. I had grown so accustomed to defending myself and my drug abuse that I got quickly offended when they asked why I failed a test after my first week of complete sobriety. I struggled all week to pass that test, and I failed? I said some words that I honestly do not remember to this day, but apparently, there was a cuss word or two involved; you do not cuss at a judge in their courtroom. I landed myself a week's vacation in the county jail plus a requirement to attend a thirty-day rehab. I felt like I was failing already, and I had just begun. I was in the program to avoid prison, but I was being sent to jail anyway. On the inside, I was freaking out because I did not see where I had gone wrong. The Drug Court coordinator must have seen it on my face because she approached me and told me that I could request my test to be sent off for lab work if I was sure it was wrong. I had forgotten that was an option due to the brain fog I was experiencing during the first days of sobriety. So I told her that I did not use, and I would like to send it off. Before the cops escorted me to the jail, my mom hugged me and told me that I needed to be praying and seeking God while I was in jail, and for the first time, I considered what she told me.

In all reality going to jail that week was exactly what my mind needed. I was able to sit and be still and not worry, and it gave me more time for the brain fog to clear. I noticed a girl reading the Bible that first night, but I was too afraid to approach anyone for anything. Then as I laid in my cell that night, I thought back to all of the stuff that my mom had been telling me all week about God. As I was thinking, I realized something was different about her; she was happy, and there was a different glow about her. I had been around her all week, and not once did I suspect that she wandered off somewhere to get high. I felt like I was going to catch her in her lies at any moment because I did not want her playing games with me.

Then I realized that maybe there is some truth to her story about God giving her freedom from drugs. At that moment, as I was lying on a one-inch mattress with an itchy blanket, I thought at this point in my life, what would it hurt if I did give it a try? What if I prayed to God and He did care and helped me get out of this mess? Because of me and my actions, my life was such a mess. So I prayed to God that night in jail and it was the first time I had since I broke down in my car about a year ago. All I asked was that He would please help me make it through this. I think the most challenging part about praying was that I had somehow felt that God was the reason my life was so messed up. I knew deep down the entire time that He was real; but I was angry about how badly I hurt, and I wanted to blame God for my pain. I had heard it said that He was real and that He created the heavens, the earth, and you and me. But here I was suffering and hurting, and it made me feel like He was not as great as people made Him out to be. But I was not looking at all the parts I played in my messed-up life. I was not looking at the fact that it was I who chose to ignore Him. I was the one who decided to live a life against His will, and it was I who decided to chase all of the things He told me through His word not to go after. I did not realize that God did not want me to participate in certain things because those were the very things that would drive me away from Him. I had seen it all wrong, and I had it all wrong in my head; but at that moment in the jail cell, I was tired of it all. I was tired of fighting a losing battle, a battle that I constantly lost. I was in a place where I had nothing else to lose.

So I prayed a simple prayer, and that is all that happened. No big light shone down from heaven, no miraculous voice spoke to me, and to be honest, nothing felt any different. But the next day, I did the same thing. I woke up and said, "God, please help me get through this." Those seven words were all that I could manage to say.

After we had breakfast, I saw the girl I had seen the night before, and she was reading the Bible again. I approached her, and I just immediately cut to the chase. I told her about my situation and all that my mom had been telling me. I cannot remember the exact words that the girl told me, but I can remember her countenance. She was happy; she was in jail, but she was happy. She had a peace over her, and it was the same peace that I had noticed over my mom. I was drawn to that happiness, and I wanted that peace.

The girl told me her story; she was a mom of two young children with a boyfriend who sold drugs. She did not even use drugs; she had never even gotten high before, but she drove across the country for her boyfriend to deliver. I just remember that while she was telling me her situation, all I could think was how there was no doubt that he used her not to get caught himself. It is somehow easier to spot other people's life issues and not our own. I felt sorry for her because she was so sweet, and I was also so blessed by her. She was godsent to me, and I had a feeling by meeting her that maybe this is what God wanted to happen.

I finished off the week in jail pretty strong because of her; she helped me find books about God to read, and she answered so many questions that I had about Him. I was not entirely convinced yet, but I was interested enough to keep pursuing Him. When I woke up, the first person I would go to was her. Each morning after breakfast, I would walk up to her cell with whatever book I was reading to talk with her.

After the week was over, my mom picked me up, and when I told her about the girl I had met, she was in tears because she was so happy. My mom told me that it was an answer to her prayers because at church, they had been praying that God would open my eyes. I just remember sitting there wondering if that is what had just happened. I mean, it was weird that my mom was praying for something I had no clue about while I was getting exactly what she was praying for, but I just was not sure yet.

I will admit my attitude was a lot better, and I could feel it. However, I still had to find a rehab center, and usually, that can take weeks. My family called different centers for me while I was in jail, but they did not have any openings yet. Finally, the same week I got out of jail, I got a call from a rehab saying I could be there a week from today. The only thing was that it was no less than forty-five days of rehab, so I had to be gone longer than I was initially ordered. I was shocked that it moved that fast; my mom told me that God was moving in my favor.

I was extremely nervous about rehab. I felt like a little kid being dropped off at a family member's house where I did not want to be for a month. I cried over leaving my dog, my special buddy, and I was scared he would not understand what happened to me. My mom's answer was always the same every time I was faced with something: "Jennie, you need to pray about it." I did not like her telling me to pray about every little problem; I wondered how talking to someone I could not even see could help me, but I continued to do it out of desperation. I prayed all the time, and it was mostly because I had no other way to cope anymore. I could not get high; I could not even smoke a cigarette in rehab, and I could not have my phone. I felt the no phone and the no cigarette rule was a little excessive, but it was obviously what I needed.

As I am writing this, I think it is so crazy how much we think we know what we need. Yet God knows exactly what we need, how we need it, and when we need it. God was in control, and I did not even know it. When I checked into rehab, I was introduced to my counselor, who did yet another assessment on my "mental status." She was very quick and bold to tell me that she was a Christian and that God was Lord over her life and that she would not apologize for speaking of Him, so I could go ahead and expect it. I just remember thinking that the entire rehab must be about God, but I learned in time that out of the three counselors there, she was the only one who talked about God.

You see, God was in control, and I was right where I needed to be every step of the way. But I could not see that at the moment. So this is just revelation as I look back at it in hindsight. I was also sent into rehab with a Bible that my mom's pastor had given to me. I was very curious about what was in it because I wanted to figure out what was really written in it. I also wanted to know what it was about God that could make people so composed, happy, and peaceful. I had to read one scripture at a time and pretty slowly because of the brain fog, which did not leave me entirely for about six months or so. So I was learning one little thing at a time and was paying attention to where it told me different things that were right or wrong in God's eyes.

During my time there, I noticed one day that the girls who were there before me all had the same kind of Bible but different from mine, and I learned that before I checked in, a group of ladies from a church brought them to rehab; the Bible was called The Life Recovery Bible. It is a Bible, just like every other Bible, but it is filled with devotions about the life of addiction. I looked through one and was immediately captivated by the idea that the Bible could actually relate to my situation and my feelings because I had no clue. It was like my every emotion and struggle was talked about page after page, and at the end of each comment, I felt hope rising inside me. I asked a girl if I could read hers at night when we had free time before lights out, and she was kind enough to lend it. I persistently read the devotionals and wrote them down because I was so encouraged. I tried to send them to Jay in prison daily so that he could see what I had just discovered.

Life in rehab turned out not to be that bad. I continued just to pray simple prayers. "God, please give me patience and help me be okay." "God, please let Busa know that I love him and that I will be back." I do not think my prayers changed much for a while, but I would catch myself praying every time I felt myself not feeling okay.

After a week went by, I was starting to feel again. I did not feel numb and angry inside. I felt like life and hope were in me, and I would even smile. I got up one morning and realized I was humming and singing along to a song in my head. I thought it was strange because I did not know what the song was, and I didn't even have access to a radio or TV to have any reason for a song to be stuck in my head. As I sang it with a few words and hummed the rest, I could not figure out what song it was. All I could come up with was, "I will stand by you." Then I would go to humming it. You know that feeling when you just cannot think of something and it bugs you? Well, that is where I was.

That afternoon I went and called Kristel, and during our conversation, she told me that she had heard a song that day, which reminded her of me and what I was going through. She said it was a song by Rascal Flatts called "I Won't Let Go." She asked me if I had heard it. I said that I could not recall hearing it but am sure I have at some point.

So the day went on, and that evening when we all had the free time to spend for ourselves, I was doing my usual, which was spending my time reading. I had just sat down to read from my friend's Life Recovery Bible when she came up to me and apologetically told me that she wanted to use her Bible that night. I told her it was no problem and that I could read my own and handed it to her.

On the other end of the room, a new girl who had just checked into rehab that morning overheard the conversation. She came up to me and said, "Hey, you can read my Bible; I have the same one that she has." I was excited as I followed her to her stuff. She added, "Just be careful with it; I have lots of notes and papers in it."

I thought to myself, "Okay, no problem." And then I saw that she was not exaggerating. Her Bible was so full of papers sticking out here and there that I was afraid even to open the book, so I carefully sat down and wondered where to even start.

I finally picked a page, and as I grabbed the paper that was in it to set it to the side, I noticed that it was song lyrics that had been printed, and it caught my attention. As I curiously started to read the lyrics, I started humming the same song that I had been singing all day, and I noticed that it had the exact words: "I will stand by you." I looked at the top of the page, and it said "I Won't Let Go" by Rascal Flatts. The same song that my sister was talking about on the phone! I immediately knew in my heart that God was speaking directly to my soul. The main words that were playing on repeat in my head that day were, "I will stand by you, I will help you through when you've done all you can do." But as I read each and every word of the song, I felt God speaking to my heart in a way that I had never felt before, and I felt His presence over me in a way I had never known possible. If you have the time, please stop and look up the lyrics online and read them to gain a fuller understanding of what God was speaking to my heart at that moment.

By the time I had finished reading it, I was almost in tears, and I was so happy I could hardly contain myself because that was a divine confirmation. God was telling me exactly what I needed to hear based on the prayers I had prayed! "God, please help me to get through this; please help me be okay." I wanted to call my mom but would not be able to until the following afternoon. I ran over to the new girl and explained what had just happened, and she thought it was pretty cool; but I did not feel that she understood the full extent of what just happened to me. The earliest that I could tell someone who would truly understand what I was experiencing was the next morning.

I just knew that I had to request to speak to my counselor, which I did the first thing that morning. I was able to go into her office, and she looked up the song; we listened to it together. She told me that she was so shocked at the life that I had in my face compared to the first day, and I felt in that moment that I finally had a taste of what I kept seeing in their lives. I had hope and peace about where I was and where I was headed. God knew what I needed to hear to touch my heart in a profound way. Just a simple confirmation that He was there with me is what I needed the most.

When God speaks to us, we cannot limit Him to only speak to us one way. God speaks to us all in many ways and differently to different people. For example, I have always had a heart for music; I love music, and when I find a good song, I can feel it in my soul. God was meeting me right where He knew it would touch my heart. I have since then had other experiences with God speaking to me through music. Some days I will wake up with a particular song playing in my heart, and I stop to listen carefully to what the lyrics are saying so that I may hear what He has to say.

Because of this spiritual awakening that day in rehab, my eyes were opened and my heart was touched, and I could immediately see how He had been with me since I cried out to Him over a year ago. He had started moving in my life the night I cried out to Him in the passenger seat of my car as I was too helpless to do anything for myself. He had mercy on me, and I am forever thankful. My eyes were opened, and I realized that every charge I had gotten and the reason they all seemed so bogus was because it was God trying to move me in a different direction. God was trying to open my eyes for a long time in a gentle way. I just chose not to acknowledge His existence, and from jail to rehab God had been with me guiding my every step.

I remembered back to a night before I had gotten sober, and I was writing to Jay when he first got put into prison and back when I thought that I was going to try the whole sobriety thing. He and I were sober for about two weeks before he went in, and it was the most peaceful time I had actually had in months. We laughed and joked, and we were happy; we did not fight. Then whenever he went in, I told him that we should continue staying sober and do something different with our lives. I was lying in bed writing and confused about everything in life, and I am truly and honestly not a born writer. I never really cared for writing, and it was not something that ever just flowed freely for me. I have always been a reader, and I appreciated other people's hard-earned wisdom. But that night, I came up with something out of the blue. I did not read it somewhere, and no one told it to me either; so I was amazed at what had come over me, and I wrote it down.

First, we have hope
Then we keep faith
Till we find the courage

I thought that I was writing this to encourage him at the moment, but it became something I grabbed ahold of and kept for myself. I wrote it down and put it away, but after God opened my eyes in rehab, I remembered these words, wrote them down, and held them close for the remainder of my time. It is another one of those hindsight moments because I did not realize this at the time, but God was speaking to my heart that night. It was not me who came up with it; God spoke these words to my heart. So I started writing this on all of my notebooks and keeping it close to me for direction and encouragement. I knew that it all started with hope, and that is what happened. By me praying, I just hoped that God would answer me, and He did. So I knew that my next step was keeping faith and believing that He is real and does hear me. And if I could do that much, then I just knew that I would have the courage to move on in life and make something of myself and overcome all of the obstacles in my path.

First, we must hope because without hope, we cannot see the future, and without hope, we will not strive toward anything. So we hope toward those things that we desire but do not yet see because a person cannot hope for something they already see.

"For we are saved in this hope, but hope that is seen is not hope; for why does one still hope for what he sees? But if we hope for what we do not see, we eagerly wait for it with perseverance."
Romans 8:24-25

Once we establish hope in our hearts, we have to keep faith that the hope in our hearts will come to pass. So then faith is what makes us sure that the things we hope for will come to pass. Then by believing that the things we hope for will come to pass, we find the courage within ourselves to step out and take new chances, and we can step out with belief in our hearts because we know that God is with us.

> *"Now faith is the substance of things hoped for, the evidence of things not seen."*
> Hebrews 11:1

> *"Have I not commanded you? Be strong and of good courage; do not be afraid, nor be dismayed, for the Lord your God is with you wherever you go."*
> Joshua 1:9

This revelation is what kept me striving toward living a sober life each day. I felt that since I had finally found the hope that I had lost so long ago, all I had to do was hold onto it and have faith in God—to faithfully believe that He was real and that He would help me find new strength each day. Then with each passing day that I held onto hope and kept my faith, I continued to not only stay sober, but I found that it was not as bad as I thought it would be. Then as time continued to pass, I found more and more courage to face the obstacles that were endlessly before me. After I had spent years of my life neglecting my responsibilities and burning bridges with my family and loved ones, I had a lot of challenges to face. Most of them seemed impossible to overcome, but I was slowly getting to where I needed to be by taking one step at a time.

One day I realized that happiness was becoming a new part of me, and I never realized just how unhappy I was in my active using until I started to feel genuine happiness in my sobriety. I realized that getting high to fulfill my happiness was not the same as genuine happiness. The happiness I sought through drugs was fake; it was a false sense of what I wanted. When I began using drugs, it was like it intensified my emotions on a good level. Like if I was having fun and then got high, I was suddenly having even more fun. Then after I used so much, my intentions changed from intensified fun to needing it to feel joy or happiness at all. But here I was, still in rehab and sober, and I had joy in my heart.

I had gone from a very noncooperative attitude to looking forward daily to doing the things that were assigned to me in rehab, all in a little over thirty days. I know that was God because it was a miracle of a difference. I searched for God in books and in the word because I wanted to see if I could find more of this happy stuff that I was feeling. I knew that it had to have been God, but I did not understand why I felt the way I did. I did not realize it at the time, but it was the life of God in me.

> *"You have made known to me the ways of life; You will make me full of joy in Your presence."*
> *Acts 2:28*

Then before I knew it, my forty-five-day rehab stay was over, and this time instead of feeling dread and gloom, I felt ready and excited to step out into the real world sober. I went back to Drug Court after coming home, and my experience was as different as black and white, and the fact that it was, made it a little more encouraging, I gained even more of the courage than I had talked about previously. I felt ready. I went from being one who complained about life and everyone involved in it to just enjoying whatever it was that I had to do. I enjoyed the required twelve-step meetings, classes, groups, and counseling that I had to do each week. I worked eagerly to do all that was required of me and more. I searched through self-help books, and I even attended extra classes as a way to pass my free time. Now, do not get me wrong, I was not on some super-high euphoric joy cloud. I still had emotions and some days were hard, but I was not the same person I was a couple of months back. I was a different person because drugs were no longer controlling my spirit. I knew that I had God in my heart, and He was living inside of me. Having God in my heart changed me and my outlook on life.

PART II

LIVING IN CHRIST & LEARNING A NEW WAY OF LIFE

GROWING IN GOD

Since the Drug Court program required that I work the twelve steps, I took them seriously and thoroughly worked them. I knew that most people would just say that they worked the steps, and then write down the answers the court wanted to hear, but they never took the actual time to work them. But I was not trying to cheat myself out of anything. In the process of working the steps, I continued to grow closer to God. I feel like working the steps helped to strengthen my relationship with God.

I know that some twelve-step programs allow individuals to choose their god and still work the same twelve steps, but that is idolatry. We should be careful not to fall into the temptation of making up a god or making up any graven image of the real God. I heard people in meetings say that they do not serve the God they learned about in church; they serve God as they know him. That makes Him into their own image, and the word plainly tells us not to do that.

> *"You shall not make for yourself a carved image—any likeness of anything that is in heaven above, or that is in the earth beneath, or that is in the water under the earth; you shall not bow down to them nor serve them. For I, the Lord your God, am a jealous God, visiting the iniquity of the fathers upon the children to the third and fourth generations of those who hate Me"*
> *Exodus 20:4-5*

In a meeting, I once heard a man say that he does not serve the God of hell, fire, and brimstone who casts judgment upon people; he would always say that his god does not judge him for how he lives his life. I did not know any different at the time, but I always felt skeptical about the whole idea of making up my own god. I know that is not biblical because although that sounds really nice, we cannot just make God into whomever we choose. The word tells us that our God is a just God and that injustice is not found in Him (Deuteronomy 32:4) and that there will be a day of judgment upon His children who choose to deny Him and live unjust lives (1 Peter 4:5, 2 Peter 2:9, Romans 14:10-11). I was also told that I could make anything I chose to be my god even if it was the doorknob. I just had to have a god to work the steps. I thought all of their opinions sounded crazy and I just chose the God I had heard about as a child and the God my mom said saved her life and the same God I was experiencing in my heart and my life. The rest seemed like nonsense to me, and I am so thankful that it did because I was able to find the *real* and living God. There is only one living God.

> *"I am the Lord, and there is none else, there is no God beside me: I girded thee, though thou hast not known me*
> *Isaiah 45:5 (KJV)*

> *"Yet I am the Lord thy God from the land of Egypt, and thou shalt know no god but me: for there is no other saviour beside me."*
> *(Hosea 13:4, KJV).*

Jesus says in John 14:6 "I am the way, the truth, and the life. No one comes to the Father except through Me." Jesus is saying that we must go through Him to get right with God, and all that consists of is that we surrender ourselves and our lives and accept Jesus Christ into our hearts as our personal Lord and Savior. It really is as easy as it sounds; we should not allow ourselves to overcomplicate something so simple, nor should we listen to the words and advice of someone who tells us what has worked for them outside of the truth of the word of God. We must heed to the word of God and do things as God's word tells us to do because otherwise it can be detrimental to true and lasting salvation. So basically, what I am saying is that I learned to not just take somebody's word for what "works" but find out through the word of God what works.

When we come to God through Jesus, He will meet us right where we are and help us get exactly where He needs us to be. Even if we come to God not knowing anything about Him, He is so patient and merciful to reveal Himself to us a little at a time in a way that we can follow. I believe that the twelve steps are designed to bring us closer to God. But just like many other things in this world, Satan has found a counterfeit way to sneak into the purpose of the steps that are meant for good and corrupt them. All I'm trying to say is this: I worked the twelve steps, and they helped me. So I would suggest the same thing for anyone else who needs them as long as they are working them to move closer toward God, the one true God.

> *"And this is life eternal, that they might know thee the only true God, and Jesus Christ, whom thou hast sent."*
> John 17:3 (KJV)

Otherwise it would only end up doing them more damage in the long run when they find out that their god has no power to save them. The thing is, I was still really messed up. I had grown accustomed to bad habits, and I had no real clue just how much of me needed change until I started working steps to change everything about my old life. I still had baggage in a manner of speaking and lots of it. But my readiness to ask God for His help every step of the way and my willingness to do what it took made the entire process a lot easier for me.

My family was all so supportive of my recovery, and my mom was always there to encourage me with the word of God. Although we were both living a new life of sobriety together, we both had different paths and journeys to take to get where God needed us to be. I was in Drug Court, so my journey was more strict and very structured, whereas her journey was entirely dependent on God. So we were involved in each other's lives, and she was always there to support me, but she was not always a part of the walk that I was on.

As I was working on step three, which had me daily focus on turning my will and my life over to the care of God, my sponsor told me to pray daily for God to show me His will. The more I prayed, the more I felt the need to let go of things and give more control to God in my life. One of those things was Jay; I realized that he was in no way a part of God's will for me and my life anymore. It was like, little by little, my eyes were opened to the truth like scales were falling off of my eyes. I could see that we were never really healthy for each other and that I deserved someone who treated me with respect.

Being in Drug Court, I was around a whole new group of people, and they were all sober. So I had new friends and I was experiencing a new life. But a big part of me did not feel like I was strong enough to do what needed to be done and break up with Jay. Every time I called him, he would somehow talk me out of doing things I wanted to do. That was the first time I had relied entirely on God to give me the words and strength to say what I had to say and do it. I will not say that it was easy because it wasn't; it still hurt, but I overcame that day by not running to something or someone else to comfort and ease my pain. Instead, I sought God through prayer. That is how I learned how I could overcome so much in my life. I just needed to look to God for strength. He has helped me to overcome drug abuse and codependency, and I share this so that others can find their hope in Him as well.

I eventually met somebody on the same road that I was on, a new life in recovery. We were both in Drug Court, and we genuinely desired to live a better life and had a lot in common. I had known Jake for almost all of my life because we were both from the same small town, but we had never had any previous dealings with each other. I quickly noticed how he and I alike desired to get through the program the best that we could without even trying to cheat the system. This caused us to click with each other in a way that we did not with anyone else. He talked about God and how he believed God had His hand in his life. We started officially dating in Drug Court, and we eventually graduated on the same day. We got married on March 22, 2014, and we have been growing in God ever since.

After God had made sobriety possible for Jake and me, we have had a consistent desire in our hearts to do better and grow in God. I do not want to portray that life was miraculously easy after finding God because that is not the case. Life will always have its challenges, and it is accurate to say that just because one finds God, it does not make life easier; it just makes it possible. At this point in my life, I had come to a place where I made a wholehearted decision never to go back to where I had come from but instead to strive forward.

My story is not over yet. God continues to fill in new chapters in my life; I know one part of my story that will never change, and that is my forever grateful heart toward Christ. I have seen God do too many miracles for me to turn from Him. I am a living testimony of God's goodness and mercy each and every day, and trust me, I need His mercies as I go because I am human and I mess up.

> *"Through the Lord's mercies we are not consumed, because His compassions fail not. They are new every morning; great is Your faithfulness."*
> Lamentations 3:22-23

Mercy is compassion or forgiveness shown toward someone who may not deserve it. Mercy is something I, as a human, have failed to show in many cases, but my Heavenly Father has never failed to show me mercy; I am thankful for it daily. Every day that I wake up is a chance to grow in God, and I do my best to embrace that opportunity. God does not expect us to wake up and just have it all together in one day. Philippians 2:13 (HCSB) says, "For it is God who is working in you, enabling you both to desire and to work out His good purpose." This is saying that God works in us and gives us the ability and the desire to do the things that He has in store for us. I have often looked upon this scripture as a reminder that progress is a process and eternal change may have happened overnight according to my destiny, but internal change is a daily process that I must desire in order to move forward. I could not and cannot allow any daily mistake or life's setbacks to determine who I am in Christ and what God has in store for my life. I must only look toward His word to define me and my life. God started to mend my heart and put my life back together the moment I surrendered my heart to Him. God is a God of restoration, and He turns ashes into beauty.

> *The Spirit of the Lord God is upon Me,*
> *Because the Lord has anointed Me*
> *To preach good tidings to the poor;*
> *He has sent Me to heal the brokenhearted,*
> *To proclaim liberty to the captives,*
> *And the opening of the prison to those who are bound;*
> *To proclaim the acceptable year of the Lord,*
> *And the day of vengeance of our God;*
> *To comfort all who mourn,*
> *To console those who mourn in Zion,*
> *To give them beauty for ashes,*
> *The oil of joy for mourning,*
> *The garment of praise for the spirit of heaviness;*
> *That they may be called trees of righteousness,*
> *The planting of the Lord, that He may be glorified.*
> *And they shall rebuild the old ruins,*

WHEN CHAINS ARE BROKEN

They shall raise up the former desolations,
And they shall repair the ruined cities,
The desolations of many generations. Isaiah 61:1-4 (KJV)

This prophecy from Isaiah came hundreds of years before Jesus, and Jesus came to fulfill it. In Luke 4:18–20, we read how Jesus proclaimed this prophecy when it was time for Him to step into His earthly ministry. Let's talk about this scripture to see precisely how Jesus has fulfilled it. The thing is that the life of an addict can accumulate a pretty big pile of disappointments, failures, brokenness, and setbacks. It is years of built-up shame, guilt, and heartache for some because using substances has turned from fun to survival. It is so easy to become bound by the chains of addiction, and then often the user does not know how to go back to any other way of life. Sadly, for some, it has been the only way they were taught to live. Addiction can be a generational curse in a family, and it can be passed from generation to generation. Without the family knowing this reality, it goes on until someone discovers this truth and declares, "It stops with me!"

But the good news is that God has sent us His Son Jesus so that we might be saved (John 3:16–17). Jesus came to heal the brokenhearted and to tell us there is freedom to those who are held captive. Jesus came to give us beauty for ashes. According to the Google dictionary, ashes are the remains of something destroyed, or ruins. In biblical times, ashes were associated with grief, humiliation, and repentance. My life, my dreams, and my plans for the future had turned to ashes because they had been completely destroyed and laid in ruins where I had left them. We all know that it is impossible to use the remains to rebuild anything once something is burned to ashes. But God can take the ashes of our mistakes and turn them into beauty.

God has made us a way through Jesus to give us joy where there has been mourning. He places a garment of praise upon us to replace the spirit of heaviness so that we may gain the strength to move forward from glory to glory. Do you know what that garment of praise means? A garment is a piece of clothing, and we wear clothing. When we have been living a life of disappointment after disappointment, we begin to live with a different type of countenance through the filter of addiction, and it becomes who we are. We wear it daily like one would wear a garment. I know that for me, I was always way more serious and never relaxed. I was always on guard, just waiting for the next person to try and mess me over because that is what everyone did. I was always disappointed in myself for disappointing my loved ones. The countenance I carried around was not a "happy, smiling, my life is going great, and I am good" countenance. It was dark and gloomy. That would be very comparable to this spirit of heaviness that is in this passage of scripture. It is saying that Jesus has come to give me a garment of praise for the spirit of heaviness. That means he will exchange my gloomy countenance and give me pure satisfaction on the inside, a satisfaction that becomes a praise that I wear.

So we grow, and we go from one level to the next. Verse four in this passage of Isaiah says, "And they shall rebuild the old ruins, They shall raise up the former desolations, And they shall repair the ruined cities, The desolations of many generations." When we go to God the Father and allow Him to work in our hearts, He gives us the strength and ability to rebuild the ruins that we have left behind us. It says that we shall raise up the former desolations. Did you know that "desolation" means complete emptiness or destruction? That is all the old stuff in our lives that we have already considered long gone and that is irreplaceable, unfixable, and never to return. This right here is talking about the ashes of our lives, the complete destruction that drugs have caused in our hearts and relationships. The ashes left behind from every mistake we have made due to drug abuse and selfish ambition can be repaired, and healing can occur in our hearts. Our broken dreams, our broken families, our broken hearts, and our broken trust can be repaired. They can be brought up through the ashes, and God can rebuild them and give them new life. But it does not just stop there. It says the desolations of many generations; God can fix things that have been going on in our families for generations! We can be that person who stands up and declares, "This stops with me! Addiction stops in my family and my bloodline!"

All of this may sound very hopeful to you, but you may be wondering, "How do I get there?" That is the simplest part of it all, and the answer is surrender. Although this is the simplest part, it is the part that we tend to make the hardest. For instance, I had to stop fighting the reality and existence of God and swallow my pride and surrender to Him. When I finally quit fighting and asked God for help, the struggle stopped and the journey began. If you were to walk into any twelve-step meeting right now, they would tell you that the first step is to admit that you are powerless and that your life has become unmanageable. It is the same thing as I have already stated: surrender.

As far as the saying "progress is a process" goes, let me just say that I never had any intention to change as much about my life as God did. But the amazing part about that is God meets us where we are, and He helps us get where we need to be one step at a time. He knows where we are in the process, and He knows what it is that we are ready to let go of or change about our lives. For example, if God had spoken to me immediately that I needed to give up smoking, I would not have been willing to give it up as I held onto smoking with a tight grip in the early stages of my sobriety. He did not place that part upon my heart until two or more years into my sobriety. If God had handed me a sheet of paper that said "Jennie, this is the list of things that I eventually want to be changed in your life," I would have probably given up before I ever started, but thankfully that is not how He works. Instead, God works with us to make us willing and able to obey Him and His purposes.

There have been times when God has spoken to my heart and I have felt convicted of a certain thing, but I was not yet willing to let go of that part of me. But I knew He was pointing it out to me for a reason, so I have learned to say the following prayer: "God, help me to want to _____." Or "God help me to want to let go of _____." Then in time, I see my heart's desires change from my own to His. It is a simple yet powerful prayer of surrender that God will honor. I cannot express how well this prayer works; only the person willing enough to try it can truly discover the power of a simple prayer of surrender.

JESUS DIED FOR US ALL

I was so blessed to have had my mom go before me because I could see with my eyes the real change that was taking place in her heart and life. It was so real that I could not deny the reality that something beyond my knowledge was taking place in her. I am thankful for her persistence in telling me that God had saved her despite my ugliness toward her at first. Without her faithfulness to God, I do not know how much longer I would have gone down the path of destruction. For this same reason, I pray that my story and journey can reach someone wherever they are and give them hope in Christ Jesus.

As I minister to people, I am too often confronted with the guilt that surrounds their souls in such a way that they feel they have done too many messed-up things to come to God. They have come to a place of complete hopelessness and feel as if they have made their bed and now they must lie in it. That is partly true but not entirely; we are still accountable for our own actions, but that does not mean that once we have messed up, we just have to stay in the bed that we have made. We can get up and remake it and start afresh, with Jesus in our hearts and lives. We must understand something: it is the broken ones who need Jesus.

> *"Jesus answered and said to them, 'Those who are well have no need of a physician, but those who are sick. I have not come to call the righteous, but sinners, to repentance."*
> *Luke 5:31–32*

The very words of Jesus Himself tell us that He came specifically for the broken because they needed healing. Jesus was sitting down with tax collectors and sinners when He spoke these words (Mark 2:15). Trust me, I know, I was very deceived on this matter as well. This is why I never sought God when my life was miserable. I knew that I did not have my life together, and "I probably did not deserve to ask Him for help." I truly felt that I could never walk through the doors of a church until I got my life together. My perception was way off, and I felt like people went to church because they did not have problems and because they had somehow done something to earn God's love. That is not how it works, and that is not how any church should be. If a church body does not accept someone who needs Jesus for healing in their hearts and lives, they are not a biblical church. I am here to tell you the truth and help correct this in hearts that have felt this same way. Believing that we do not belong in church or that we are not worthy to come to God is a lie and a deception that the enemy wants us to believe to keep us from true deliverance. Jesus came for us all, not just a select few, and despite what you think right now, I am here also to tell you that no one can be right standing with God by what they do. We become right standing with God by our faith in His Son Jesus Christ.

> *"Knowing that a man is not justified by the works of the law but by faith in Jesus Christ, even we have believed in Christ Jesus, that we might be justified by faith in Christ and not by the works of the law; for by the works of the law no flesh shall be justified."*
> Galatians 2:16

If we were to step back and take a look directly into the ministry of Jesus, we would find that He ministered to the outcasts of society. I have already mentioned how He dined with tax collectors, who were known as the traitors of their day. The Jews were under Roman rule, and the tax collectors were Jews who worked for the Romans to collect money from the Jews for the Romans. So the Jews saw them as traitors to their own country. Who would have known that Jesus himself sought and ministered the love of the Father to those who were known in society as traitors?

We also read in John 4 of the woman at the well. Jesus knew what He was doing when He went to that particular well that day. He knew there would be a woman in search of water who not only needed her physical thirst quenched but even more she had a thirst in her soul that could not be quenched by any earthly means. She needed a drink from the eternal and life-giving water that can only come from above. Is that not just like you and me? Have we not searched high and low throughout life for something to satisfy our souls, only to wake up each morning still hungry or thirsty for another thrill or another high?

I searched for satisfaction and fulfillment in people, but they would only let me down. I searched for fulfillment in drugs and alcohol, but they would always run out. I searched for fulfillment in my abilities, talents, and accomplishments in life, but they were never enough. This woman that Jesus met at the well was not just any woman; she was a woman with a past, a past with men and a past of hurt. The fact that she had gone through five husbands and was currently living with another man can easily show us that she, too, looked for fulfillment from people in her life. The people of the law in that day just looked down on her for the life that she lived, but Jesus wanted to give life to her soul. The text says in verse six that it was about the sixth hour, which means that it was about noon. This indicates that it was in the heat of the day when the woman came to draw the water from the well. The fact that she is alone and is coming at the heat of the day shows that this woman is an outcast to those around her. The other women of the town would have already drawn their water before the heat of the day. I say all of this to tell you that just because you may not fit in with the rest of the people in your family or your town does not make you any less in God's eyes. Just because you may be the black sheep of your family due to all of the mistakes that you have made does not mean that God thinks you are too messed up to become a part of His flock. God wants you to be a part of His family, and He sent Jesus to tell us just how much He wants us. Just as Jesus told the woman at the well: "Whoever drinks of this water will thirst again, but whoever drinks of the water that I shall give him will never thirst. But the water that I shall give him will become in him a fountain of water springing up into everlasting life," He has come to tell you and me the same thing. If we continue searching for internal satisfaction by the world's ways, we will always continue to search because we will never truly be satisfied. But if we go to God the Father through Jesus Christ, we can be fulfilled with satisfaction that never runs out. Just as Jesus came for the outcast woman at the well, Jesus has come for you and me.

We read of many instances in the Bible where Jesus ministered to outcasts like the criminal (Luke 19:1–7, Acts 9), the adulterer (John 4:1–26, John 8:3–4), and the physically and mentally ill (Mark 1:40–41, Matthew 8:28–33). Forget your perception of Jesus and what you have assumed to be true. Read the Bible and find what is really true about Jesus and what He has come for, and see for yourself that it is you and me that He has come to save and to heal.

"I have not come to call the righteous, but sinners, to repentance."
Luke 5:32

Another one of the questions and doubts that I come across the most as I minister is this: "What if I have done too many messed-up things?" See, many people may understand that Jesus has come to save the lost and give them life, but they do not feel like they deserve it due to the things they have done in their addiction. They feel as if there is no possible way God would even want to forgive them. But that is a lie because God loves us all so much that He gave us His only Son that we might be saved, and Jesus loves us so much that He willingly gave us His life, even while we were still sinners.

> *"For God so loved the world, that He gave His only begotten Son, that whoever believes in Him should not perish but have everlasting life. For God did not send His Son into the world to condemn the world, but that the world through Him might be saved."*
> *John 3:16-17*

> *By this we know love, because He laid down His life for us. And we also ought to lay down our lives for the brethren."*
> *1 John 3:16*

God has chosen us before the foundation of the world (Ephesians 1:4-6) God has known us since the very beginning of life (Psalm139:13-18, Jeremiah 1:5). Just as a mother expectingly loves their baby in the womb, God has loved you and me. But even if we have never followed God in our lives and even if we have gone down the wrong path and messed up, God still loves us.

> *But God demonstrates His own love toward us, in that while we were still sinners, Christ died for us."*
> *Romans 5:8*

Jesus had the sinners (you and me) on His heart while He hung on the cross. And He did it to make way for them to be saved. God has loved you this whole time; it does not matter what kind of life you have lived, and it does not matter what kind of things you have done in your past because He has an everlasting love toward His children.

> *Who shall separate us from the love of Christ? Shall tribulation, or distress, or persecution, or famine, or nakedness, or peril, or sword? As it is written: "For Your sake we are killed all day long; We are accounted as sheep for the slaughter." Yet in all these things we are*

> *more than conquerors through Him who loved us. For I am persuaded that neither death nor life, nor angels nor principalities nor powers, nor things present nor things to come, nor height nor depth, nor any other created things, shall be able to separate us from the love of God which is in Christ Jesus or Lord.*
> Romans 8:35-38

This passage of scripture talks about how no one or nothing can separate us from the love of Christ—no power on earth, no demon in hell, nor any action that we have done. We go through life and things happen, situations arise, and people or demon spirits sometimes come against us, but no matter what it is, God will not change His heart toward us even if we mess up. God is not human, so we cannot compare Him to humans (Numbers 23:19). Through experience with all of the times I messed up and hurt people, it was harder for them to show love toward me because my actions hurt them. In the same way when someone hurt me, I would naturally separate my feelings toward them and no longer care for them the way I did because I am human and I was trying to protect my broken heart. We can rest assured that God does not do that. Because I have accepted His Son Jesus into my heart and asked for His forgiveness of my sins, He is willing to overlook the things that I have put myself through and overlook the things that I have done against others and Him and still feel the deep love that He has for me. This goes hand in hand with a repentant heart and the acceptance of His Son on our end; we must accept Jesus Christ into our hearts and our lives, and we must repent of the sins we have committed. And once we do, He no longer sees the sin. He sees His child and the potential we have in Him.

The passage that we just read pertained to me in so many ways because I had come into sobriety with so many things I had done, and most of it, I had hoped no one would ever know about me. I had a heart that was so full of shame, and I had a lot of pain that I had buried deep inside because I had masked them with drugs for so long. Then even as I got sober, I still went through things and did some pretty messed-up stuff, but at the time, I did not know any better. So when I had first realized that God loved me no matter what, it was kind of hard to believe. Maybe it was hard to believe because even I did not love me. Satan wants nothing more than to make us believe that the mistakes we made are unredeemable and that there is no way God still loves us, but we must realize that is a lie. The word says that no power, principality (a ruler of darkness), or anyone (even Satan) can separate us from His love. So even if we gave our souls to the devil and served him for drugs most of our life, God still loves us, and He waits for us to come to Him. As a matter of fact, God loves His children so much that it passes our knowledge (Ephesians 3:19). Our minds cannot even grasp the reality of His love for us. So if we could just believe that He loves us despite our past, we can move forward and grow into the children God has created us to be.

WHERE TO BEGIN

So now that we know that Jesus has died for us, and God still loves us, maybe you are wondering how to start a new life. To start a new life in Him, we must first and foremost have Jesus Christ in our hearts as our personal Lord and Savior.

> *"If you confess with your mouth the Lord Jesus and believe in your heart that God has raised Him from the dead, you will be saved. For with the heart one believes unto righteousness, and with the mouth confession is made unto salvation."*
> Romans 10:9-10

This passage tells us that all we must do is pray a prayer of faith, stating that we believe that Jesus is Lord and that He not only died on the cross for our sins but that He also rose from the grave and is alive today. (I have written a salvation prayer for anyone who may need it in the back of the book.) Once we have accepted Jesus in our hearts, we can now begin a journey toward freedom from all the weight of sin, shame, and guilt that has built up throughout our drug abuse. But, first, we must confess our sins to God so that we can be forgiven and set free from them (Acts 2:38, 17:30). Once we repent of our sins, our faithful Father will forgive us and cleanse us from our unrighteousness.

> *"If we confess our sins, He is faithful and just to forgive us our sins and to cleanse us from all unrighteousness."*
> 1 John 1:9

I know it sounds too simple to be true, but it is true and that simple. To repent means that we first feel bad for our behavior, and then we follow it up with action by ceasing or stopping that activity in our lives. It is not true repentance if we do not have enough remorse to try and change our behaviors. Like for me, the first three times I got arrested, I told my loved ones that I was sorry for all of the trouble I was causing them, but the truth is that I was not really sorry because if I were, I would have stopped the behavior to prevent myself from getting arrested. I was finally sorry to God and my family once I was sober long enough that my mind was clear and my eyes were opened to see the pain and trouble I was causing everyone, including myself. When our hearts become truly repentant, we do not need to worry if God believes us or not because He knows the heart (Psalm 44:21).

Once we have Jesus in our hearts and have confessed our sins to God, the healing process will begin within us. It will be a process, and change will begin immediately within our hearts. But we must realize that we have spent years getting to the place we left off, so it may take a little time to change old behavior patterns. However, we can rest confidently knowing that Christ now lives within us, and through Him, we will have the strength and ability to overcome things we have never been able to.

"Therefore, if anyone is in Christ, he is a new creation; old things have passed away; behold, all things have become new."
2 Corinthians 5:17

In Christ, we become new creations, and in God's eyes, He no longer sees us as the world sees us. He sees us for what He created us to be, and that is His child who has a purpose and a destiny here on this earth. For me, I just knew that inside I was someone completely different. I did not feel like I was the old Jennie, and I knew in my heart that God changed something in me because of how I had experienced him. But I had trouble behaving much differently on the outside because I did not know any different way to behave. I had to learn. I had to learn little by little how to live right. My negative impulses were still there, but by seeking Him through prayer and reading His Word, I learned a step at a time how God would desire me to cope with life and how I could better handle certain situations. The Word of God is how we are transformed from the inside out.

> *"And do not be conformed to this world, but be transformed by the renewing of your mind, that you may prove what is that good and acceptable and perfect will of God."*
> *Romans 12:2*

The way that our minds can be renewed is through the Word of God. My journey began solely based on God and His Word. My mom gave me godly advice and encouragement, but I did not start going to church regularly until later in my sobriety. Although that was the case for me, I do not suggest that at all because fellowship with other believers greatly benefits us and brings us encouragement and guidance. I was just so involved in the Drug Court program, and it kept me so focused and busy on the things I had to do for the program that I was really sporadic with my church attendance. Although it was in that way that I learned to rely on God at a very personal level from the beginning, it was not until I was regular with my church attendance that I truly began to grow the most. It was not just going to church that caused me to grow but also through reading His Word and the guidance of the Holy Spirit that I was taught how to live right for Him and not as the world lives. But as I regularly attended church service, my passion and hunger for God intensified, and I grew even closer and more committed as a result.

> *I did my best to obey God as I learned more about Him through His word, but there were times when I failed, and*

*there are still days I fall short of where I need to be. "For
all have sinned, and come short of the glory of God."
Romans 3:23 (KJV)*

God knows that I am not perfect, and none of us are, but that is where His mercy comes in and He reveals to us His compassion for us and our lives. I say this all lightly because it is true for those genuinely trying to grow in Him and His will for their lives. Our God is a compassionate God.

*"The Lord is gracious and full of compassion, Slow to
anger and great in mercy. The Lord is good to all, And
His tender mercies are over all His works."
Psalms 145:8-9*

The definition of compassion is sympathetic pity and concern for the sufferings or misfortunes of others. But that does not mean that we can play the whole "ignorance is bliss" card and just assume that He will keep forgiving us when we mess up as we keep living life the way we choose because we did not "know" any better. God's Word mentions that His children are destroyed for their lack of knowledge (Hosea 4:6). Ignorance can lead to destruction in our lives, and it can lead us to shame, guilt, and wrong turns. His mercies will cover us as our hearts are right toward Him and when we feel remorse for our mistakes, not when we choose not to learn His will and His way. As we do our part and read the word of God and learn who He is and learn how He desires us to live, He will lovingly and mercifully direct us and keep us.

The world will tell us how to live our lives all day long, but the thing is, what the world views as right and wrong does not always align with the word of God. I learned in God's word that abortion is not okay in His eyes. The world told me that it was okay and that it was my choice to make. The world encouraged me to make a self-righteous decision based on my reasonings. The Word of God would have told me differently, and if I had known it, I could have saved myself from a whole lot of shame and guilt. But thankfully, His word also taught me that because of Jesus, when I confess my sins and mistakes to God, I am shown mercy, and I am forgiven.

"He who covers his sins will not prosper, but whoever confesses and forsakes them will have mercy."
Proverbs 28:13

"I acknowledged my sin to You, And my iniquity I have not hidden. I said, "I will confess my transgressions to the Lord," And You forgave the iniquity of my sin."
Psalm 32:5

"In Him we have redemption through his blood, the forgiveness of sins, according to the riches of His grace."
Ephesians 1:7

As I have previously mentioned, His word also taught me that through Jesus Christ, I am a new creation, so according to God, the old me and my past mistakes do not define who I am today.

"Therefore, if anyone is in Christ, he is a new creation; old things have passed away; behold, all things have become new."
2 Corinthians 5:17

The word also taught me that once I have accepted Jesus Christ into my heart as my personal Lord and Savior and have become His new creation, I am not condemned for my past.

"There is therefore now no condemnation to those who are in Christ Jesus, who do not walk according to the flesh, but according to the Spirit."
Romans 8:1

To condemn means to express very strong disapproval or to pronounce someone guilty. God does not pronounce me guilty to be punished now because I have given my heart to His Son and asked for forgiveness. Satan loves to make Christians feel as if God does not forgive or forget certain things about their past, and due to their lack of knowledge, Satan continues to hold many in the bondage of condemnation. But the word is clear here, and it says that God does forgive me and I am right with Him. Through His word, I have continuously reminded myself that no mistake that I have ever made can separate me from His love (Romans 8:38-39). From the moment that I surrendered my heart and my life to God and accepted Jesus into my heart, Jesus cleansed me from all of my sins, and He still does. Do not take this all wrong; do not think I did not suffer from pain and regret because I did. It took me time to realize all of these truths. I had to seek God and receive His healing for a time, but once I learned these truths in His Word, I was set free.

"And ye shall know the truth, and the truth shall make you free."
John 8:32 (KJV)

His truth is what sets us free. I honestly contemplated sharing this part of me for the world to see because it has always just been between God and me, but my heart is to share my testimony to give hope to anyone who has lost theirs. So if this part of my story can encourage or help even one person, then for the glory of God, I am willing to share my mistakes so that they may be encouraged. God loves us all, and Jesus has already paid the price to set us free from all hurt and all chains. If this pertains to you somehow, I pray that you will find freedom today.

THE JOURNEY

Each of us differ in our backgrounds and lifestyles before and during our drug abuse. The place that many call rock bottom will be different for every person as well. We are all uniquely different in our lives and personalities, and what may have been my rock bottom may not have even fazed another. We cannot judge one person to the next on what they call rock bottom. Rock bottom refers to a time or an event in life that causes an addict to reach the lowest possible point in his addiction. It is a time when the person finally feels like things cannot get any worse.

So the main thing we all have in common is that we are hurting or have been hurt due to the repercussions of our drug abuse. I think we will all know inside when we have hit rock bottom. If you are still questioning whether or not you have reached it, then it is possible that you have not. If that is the case, then I pray that you will take a moment with God to ask Him to help you define where you are right now as your rock bottom because the reality is that it could always get worse. It does not matter how bad it is for you right now—somehow, it could always get worse. If you have not come to a place where you are so beyond sick and tired of feeling sick and tired, it can and will continue getting worse. I think that is where the insanity part of addiction comes in. We keep going out and expecting that things will somehow fix themselves or just work out. But if we are not making any direct changes in our lives, the results will continue to be the same. I have heard many times before in twelve-step recovery meetings that the definition of insanity is doing the same thing over and over and expecting different results. That honestly makes a lot of sense when you look at it that way. I mean, why would we expect something to turn out any differently if we never change our actions or behavior? If I were coloring a picture and used blue for what is supposed to be the grass and realized that it did not look green, why would I keep grabbing different shades of blue to reach my desired green grass? I wouldn't, or at least I shouldn't, because that would just be crazy, right? There is a passage of scripture that makes me think of the insanity cycle of addiction.

> "But it has happened to them according to the true proverb: 'A dog returns to his own vomit,' and, 'a sow, having washed, to her wallowing in the mire.'"
> 2 Peter 2:22

I was reading this one day, and I thought to myself, "Wow, this is exactly how I was in my addiction!" First, I would get arrested, and then I would promise my family and loved ones that I was sorry and that I would not do it again. Then as soon as I got out, I would go right back to doing everything I was doing before I got arrested. I would lie to people just to cover up my actions and then get caught in my own web of lies. Then, in an attempt to fix everything that I messed up, I would promise never to do it again. As soon as I convinced them that I was sorry, I would go back to lying. I would do some ignorant things, get caught, say I am sorry, and then repeat it over and over just because I somehow convinced myself that the results would not be the same. That is insanity! I just kept on coloring my grass with a blue crayon and expected it to turn out green.

I have always wondered why dogs eat their own vomit. Not only is it nasty but, really, why would you return to something that made you so sick inside? Why would you risk putting that back inside of you? So why would we return to something (drugs) that destroys everything inside of us? Why would we risk losing our family again? Why would we risk losing our jobs and homes over and over again? Isn't once enough? Isn't one heartbreak enough? Isn't one loss enough? It does not matter who you are, how long you have used, or how little you have lost because it will always catch up with you until eventually you lose it all.

You must learn to stop the comparison game because it does not matter who else is worse off than you are. What matters is your life and what you do with it. There must come a time and a place that we stop returning to the things that destroy us. Stop expecting different results! The results may not always look the same, but I can promise you, it is all vomit! My point is that if you do not feel that you are at your rock bottom, then you need to be considering all that drugs have taken from you and then consider all that they can still take from you. I also advise never to underestimate the ability and power drugs have to take all we love or have ever held close. If you do not see it, then find your rock bottom before it is too late.

Through trial and error, I have had to learn not to compare my deliverance and my walk with God with others around me. It seems so natural to the man who walks with the world to do things how everyone else is doing it, but that is not how God works. What I mean by the world is those who live for themselves and their selfish desires, doing things the world's way and not God's way. People of the world are not allowing God to be over their hearts or their lives. When I lived my life of active using, I was of the world, but now that I have accepted Jesus Christ into my heart as my personal Lord and Savior, I am no longer a part of this world. I am just here temporarily. I now live for God, and His ways are not the world's ways (Isaiah 55:8), so I cannot expect God to do things the same way that the world does.

God's ways are extraordinarily different than what one is used to doing in following the world's ways. He works with each individual differently, and He personally ministers to us as each person needs. Because of this, I cannot expect God to minister to me the same way that he does you. Just like when I first found God through my personal experience in rehab, He spoke to me through music. Music was and is something very personal and dear to me. I had and still have a heart for music, and many times since then, God has spoken to my heart through music. I hear lyrics to a song, and I know unquestionably that God is speaking to my heart. I cannot explain it. I just know with my heart. Then there are still times when I wake up in the morning with a new song in my heart; it is one I have not even listened to recently, so I pay careful attention to the lyrics because I know that it may be God speaking to me. Although music is the most common way God speaks to me, it is not the only way. I have dreams that God gives me as well. I figured out all of this pretty early on in my walk with God because it happened time and time again. I can see how God has placed the gift of dreaming in me since I was a child because I have always been a very vivid dreamer. As a child, there were many times Satan had tried to distract this gift in me by giving me nightmares, but it is something that God had placed in me since the beginning; it was to be used for Him.

In the same way that we are all different people, we all have different gifts placed in us to suit our callings. And the point that I am trying to make is we cannot compare. We cannot compare our deliverance, our gifts, or our ability to hear God. Because if we do, we will miss our own deliverance and our own gifts, and we won't hear when God is actually speaking to us. There was a season in my walk where I missed it because I was constantly comparing. I had good intentions because I was just so desperate for God in a way that I had not ever desired Him, but I was too focused on how He was moving and speaking to other people that I could not hear Him trying to speak to me. For a season, I dismissed the idea that God would speak to me through music and focused solely on how amazing it was that He spoke to so-and-so in a certain way. I longed just to hear God's voice half as much as they did, and somehow I lost focus on how God spoke to me directly. It is like a language. If you speak to someone in a language they do not understand, they will not know what you are trying to tell them. I had somehow put aside my love language with God. It may have taken me a while to realize it, but once I realized that God does speak to us all differently, I stopped comparing, and I could hear from Him more.

The more time we spend with God, the more we will learn who He is and how He speaks to us uniquely. But one thing is certain, God will always speak to us through His Word, and God will always use the Holy Spirit to teach us and remind us of what He has said through His Word (John 14:26). The Holy Spirit teaches us how to grow and change. God will speak to us through other people as well. He will orchestrate it perfectly so that the right person is in the right place at the right time with the right words that speak to our hearts and our situation. Other times your pastor may give you a message, and it will speak directly to your heart and situation, all without your pastor knowing what you were even going through. These are all ways that God speaks to us, but never get caught in the trap of thinking that God has to speak to you the same way He speaks to someone else.

Be open to being different from other people so that you do not miss what God has in store specifically for you. In the Bible, God spoke to Mary, the mother of Jesus, through the angel Gabriel (Luke 1:26–38). Then God spoke to Joseph, whom she was to marry, through an angel in his dream (Matthew 1:20-21, 2:13). Yet God spoke to Jonah directly (Jonah 1: 1-2) and indirectly through the circumstances surrounding him(Jonah 1:4-17). God spoke to many people differently throughout the Bible. I believe that God reaches each person according to their understanding and personality. I know that was the case for me when God caught my attention by speaking to me through music. He knew I already had a heart for it and that I would have an ear for it as well.

We cannot compare how God will deliver us because God has something unique for us in deliverance too. There are so many different ways that God has delivered His people. He is an awesome God, and we cannot put Him into a box of expectations to only work a certain way because that would be limiting a limitless God. I watched my mom change before my eyes as far as using drugs was concerned. Even though she and I were not talking when she got saved, I never once heard her tell me that getting sober or staying sober was a struggle. She just did it, and she did it with a happy heart. I know that is because she laid her heart out before God, and God delivered her from the bondage of addiction. She never once needed a twelve-step recovery program, and she never needed rehab.

Then there is someone like me, who was forced into sobriety. I followed the advice to seek God because I was so desperate to feel okay that I accidentally found Him. I have seen some come to church with a desire to change, but no real changes occurred immediately; it may have taken them a little bit longer, but they finally did. I feel that is the case for some because they were not at a place of complete surrender, and that is because they were choosing to keep one foot in the world and trying to follow God with the other; it will not work that way. Because of this, many have dragged the deliverance process for months and, in some cases, years. But the moment they had finally had enough and truly surrendered their hearts and lives to God, it was like overnight their whole life changed and their families were restored.

I have seen couples with marriages falling apart due to addiction come in with a desperate cry for help, and God restored everything in their life that the enemy had stolen, plus some. One person I know went from getting high and selling drugs one day to witnessing the love of Jesus Christ to the people who came to buy drugs, trying to get them saved the very next day. But the most significant part about our deliverance is our surrender and how much we are willing to give God.

Look at it this way: our lives are one big puzzle. Through the destruction of our addictive lifestyle, our puzzle has not only been taken apart but thrown about, tossed here and there, and we are eventually left with a million pieces of our hearts and lives shattered and broken. Then when we take a step back and look at all the mess, we have no clue where to start. We may attempt to begin placing it back together on our own, but we soon find out that it is just too big of a mess to handle; we fall back into the same destructive patterns as before. But if we go to God and give Him the innermost cries of our hearts and the scattered and broken pieces of our puzzle (life), He will start putting some of the pieces back together for us. Other pieces He may hand to us and show us where to place them.

Nonetheless, the more we surrender or allow Him to piece things together for us, we eventually, piece by piece, will have our puzzle (life) back together. But if we do not allow Him to have certain pieces of our lives, how can He piece it back together? If we hold on to this hurt and that memory or certain pleasures, how can our puzzle (or life) ever be completed? It will not be completed until we surrender it all to God. We cannot hold on to any pieces for any reason, or it will end up tripping us up because our hearts and lives were never completely put back together or mended.

Our stories and testimonies are all different, and God intends them that way to reach different people. We read in Exodus 14 how God delivered the Israelites from their pursuing enemies, the Egyptians, in a miraculous way with the parting of the Red Sea. In Jonah chapter 2, we read how he was literally experiencing hell due to his actions, yet God still delivered him when he cried out to Him. God caused the fish that swallowed him to vomit him out. Then we read of Saul before he became the Apostle Paul, which is my favorite deliverance story in the Bible.

> *Then Saul, still breathing threats and murder against the disciples of the Lord, went to the high priest and asked letters from him to the synagogues of Damascus, so that if he found any who were of the Way, whether men or*

> *women, he might bring them bound to Jerusalem. As he journeyed, he came near Damascus, and suddenly a light shone around him from heaven. Then he fell to the ground and heard a voice saying to him, "Saul, Saul, why are you persecuting Me?" And he said, "Who are You, Lord?" Then the Lord said, "I am Jesus, whom you are persecuting. It is hard for you to kick against the goads." So he, trembling and astonished, said, "Lord, what do You want me to do?" Then the Lord said to him, "Arise and go into the city, and you will be told what you must do." And the men who journeyed with him stood speechless, hearing a voice but seeing no one. Then Saul arose from the ground, and when his eyes were opened he saw no one. But they led him by the hand and brought him into Damascus. And he was three days without sight, and neither ate nor drank. (Acts 9:1–9)*

Saul was a religious leader who was on a direct mission to persecute anyone who believed in Jesus. He had a self-righteous attitude with "good intentions." Saul believed in God and His laws, but he did not believe that Jesus really was who He said He was. As Saul was on the road and in the middle of his self-willed mission, Jesus stopped him in his tracks by suddenly shining a bright light upon Saul. As Saul heard a voice, he responded by asking who it was. The reply was that it was Jesus Himself! Up to that very moment, Saul did not believe in the Son Jesus Christ, and then all of a sudden, Jesus was speaking to him!

As we read this in black and white, it is easy to think well this is so obvious because Jesus revealed himself to Saul in a miraculous way. It is no wonder that Saul changed his heart and his life and decided to follow Jesus. The first time I read this, I wondered why God did not just do something to me miraculously so that I could have been saved as a result and had my life changed so much sooner?

That is when God so clearly spoke to my heart and said, "Jennie, I did reveal myself to you. Many times. But you chose to ignore me."

    Wow, I stopped in my thoughts and sat astonished because the words I felt the Lord speak went directly to my heart and struck me at the core. I spent a moment and thought back to all of the times God did try to reveal himself to me and all of the times I purposefully ignored Him, such as when God answered my prayer as a kid and I chose to run from Him. I had experienced two car wrecks in the midst of my reckless living. One was when I was a young teenager due to drinking, and the other one that I had mentioned earlier; I survived the wreck each time. Logically, there is no possible way I should have survived either of the two without some kind of supernatural intervention. Then, I survived an overdose; logically, I should have died, but I did not. He was there every time I landed myself in jail, trying to slow me down long enough to open my eyes so that I could see the life I was living and what I was doing to myself. God does not hide from us. He reveals Himself to us daily because He desires for us to know Him.

> *"For since the creation of the world His invisible attributes are clearly seen, being understood by the things that are made, even His eternal power and Godhead, so that they are without excuse,"*
> *Romans 1:20*

    Stop and think about the sunset, the mountains, the ocean, the gestation of a child in a mother's womb, the galaxy. These are all beautiful and unexplainable mysteries of this world; they are marvelous and so spectacular that scientists may have come up with many names and reasons as to why things happen, but they do not fully understand the true existence of how or why things are that way, in the beginning. I mean, sure, they can explain all there is to the gestation cycle of a mother carrying a child because they have studied it, but if you really think of it, how miraculous is it that a human is formed from an embryo? Or that entire fruit-producing trees are created from one tiny seed? We cannot even get started on all that God has done in the depths of the ocean because the ocean is so deep and vast that scientists cannot explore it all to come up with scientific reasons and explanations for it all. The galaxy is beyond comprehension as it is still beyond human intelligence today. All of these things go to prove that something more significant and unique has created it all. God has given us the beauty of the world around us to see that He is God, the creator of the universe and man. So when I had this revelation that God had been showing Himself to me the entire time, my whole heart flooded with gratitude that He never gave up on me. Any average human would have already given up all hope in me, and most had, but God never did. He loved me unconditionally and never stopped.

One other thing that I noticed about Saul was that he was not compelled or driven by any force to obey Jesus besides his own free will. I read this story many times and assumed that Saul had no other choice than to obey Jesus, but that is not the case. After Jesus revealed who he was, Saul, trembling and astonished, asked, "Lord, what do you want me to do?" Jesus answered by saying, "Arise and go into the city, and you will be told what you must do." So Saul was given a choice; he was not forced to go anywhere. But what happened is that he had an obvious encounter with the Lord, and Saul was desperate to know what to do to get where he needed to be; the Lord was faithful to answer. When I minister this story, I call this the "fork in the road moment." At this exact moment in Saul's life, he had a choice to make. He could go into the city where the Lord had told him to go, or he could continue going his own way. When the Lord intervenes in our life, we too have a choice, and our decision can ultimately be a life-or-death choice, especially living in the midst of an addiction-filled life.

I came to a place where I could finally see how I had a choice when I cried out to God that night in my car. I could have chosen to follow the peace that He had given me and pursue Him further, but I didn't. If I had been wise, I would have prayed to Him again when I returned to my apartment that night and sought Him for further strength and direction. The day my family showed up to take me home, I could have seized the opportunity to follow God's leading because I know in my heart that day was a God move. But because things seemed to be going well, I decided to keep my life in my own hands and try to force the outcome that I desired. That was not the only time in my life that I was at a fork in the road. There were several of them, and repeatedly I chose the wrong path. But I praise God for His enduring love that keeps pursuing us because it is not His will for any to perish but that all would come to repentance (2 Peter 3:9).

I would like to point out one more thing. The Lord did not tell Saul what was going to happen next either. All that Jesus said was, "Arise and go into the city, and you will be told what you must do." One thing about following God is that He will not always give us all the answers we want when we want them. God will never leave us lost and confused because His Word tells us that He will never leave us or forsake us (Deuteronomy 31:6, Hebrews 13:5). But there are many times that He will give us one instruction or one step at a time, and as we listen, He will reveal the next step. Just like Jesus did with Saul, as Saul obeyed and went into the city, the Lord had already made provision for Saul to have his sight restored (Acts 9:10–18). As we take steps of obedience toward God, He will open our eyes to the truth that sets us free (John 8:32).

I believe God works this way for a few reasons. First, we learn to rely on and trust in Him with our lives. Second, we may get too far ahead of ourselves and try to skip necessary steps to get to where our ultimate goal is faster. And third, we may run in the opposite direction due to our lack of belief in what God can accomplish in and through us. God knows what is best for us, and so whatever the reason is that God only gives us a step at a time, we should trust that it is for our good.

We can learn many great lessons from Saul here. Because Saul was willing to obey the Lord and go into the city and wait for his next direction, God was able to use him in a mighty way. Saul became known as Paul (Acts 13:9), and he wrote thirteen books of the New Testament; He came all the way from persecuting anyone who believed in Jesus to a mighty man of God. So do not for one minute think that your past failures and mistakes are too much for God to not turn into something that can bring glory to His name. This is just one of the many testimonies of deliverance in the Bible. God is a God of deliverance, and although each deliverance story is unique, they all have the same goal: God saving them from something when they could not save themselves. Deliverance is the beautiful beginning of so much more, as in the life of Saul, who became Apostle Paul. God can turn every single failure and past sin into something that can be used for the advancement of His kingdom here on earth. That is how our God works.

When I was on the outside looking in, I thought that the people in churches were the ones who had it all together. You know—all the pastors, singers, authors, and speakers—yeah, I thought they were the smart ones with good educations and the ones who already had a good name for themselves. I thought they were the ones who must have always known God and grew up in church and went to college and then got married and had kids. I did not feel as if they were perfect necessarily, but I definitely thought that they had worked hard all their life to be used by God. But I had no clue that I had it entirely wrong.

> *Brothers, consider your calling: Not many are wise from a human perspective, not many powerful, not many of noble birth. Instead, God has chosen what is foolish in the world to shame the wise, and God has chosen what is weak in the world to shame the strong. God has chosen what is insignificant and despised in the world—what is*

viewed as nothing—to bring to nothing what is viewed as something, so that no one can boast in His presence. But it is from Him that you are in Christ Jesus, who became God-given wisdom for us—our righteousness, sanctification, and redemption, in order that, as it is written: The one who boasts must boast in the Lord. (1 Corinthians 1:26–31, HCSB)

This passage of scripture explains to us how God uses those who the world would never think twice to use. God will take those considered "foolish" by the world, and He will use them in mighty ways. I know that the world around me considered me foolish, for good reasons, because I was. I wasted everything that the Lord had blessed me with and traded it for drugs. I was not doing anything with my life except wasting away every day getting high. Yet God chose me. The word says that God will choose the weak, insignificant, and despised and turn them all into someone with His glory and power so that the world will know that it was God and his power and not their strength and ability. It assures me that God will continue to turn my story into something mighty just like He did for Saul. These scriptures highly encourage me, and with each new level that I have taken with God, I have stood on this passage to know that even if I do not feel qualified for something, it does not mean that God is not equipping me to do the task He has placed in my heart. When I first got saved, I knew this passage of scripture meant that the world may still see me as foolish, but God wants to use me. Then when God placed it upon my heart to start ministering in the jails, I had no education as far as the world's standards, but I did have knowledge of the Word I had been reading; I knew that if God placed it on my heart, then he would help me to minister.

When God placed it on my heart to write my testimony in a book, I knew that technically I was not qualified to do so. I don't have any college education that has taught me how to write, and after years of not paying attention to how I speak, I have formed bad grammatical habits. But I knew that if God had placed it upon my heart, He would equip me, and He would get all of the glory for it. This way I may boast in Him, and the Glory of God will be revealed.

When I started to feel led to write my testimony, I had a dream one night that I will never forget. In my dream, I just remember standing there when I suddenly saw big hands hand me something that looked much like a tablet. I reached forward to grab it, and as soon as I did, the hands went away; I could see something before me. I looked ahead of me, and I could see that God had called me to do something that I would never have dreamed of doing. It is challenging to explain because it does not always make sense to the natural mind the things God shows us in dreams. But when He does give us dreams, the Holy Spirit will reveal to our hearts what God is showing us, and without logical explanation, we just know that we know what God is saying. We must be careful to prayerfully seek God about a dream because not all dreams are from Him. But when I looked up in my dream, I remember feeling emotions. I felt shocked that God was calling me to do this, yet I felt confident because God had just given me what I needed to step into that calling.

When I woke up, I knew that it was confirmation to start writing this book. Because I would never have imagined myself writing a book. But God! So be encouraged, my dear friend, that as long as you walk with God, you do not need to care what the world thinks of you or how the world measures you because God has a plan for you.

MADE FOR VICTORY

I recently cleaned out some stuff in my bedside drawer, and I found one of my older daily journals. I have kept a daily journal for the last fifteen years, and it is nothing big and detailed. It is just a small account as to what I did that day in a yearly planner. I found one from the year 2009 and just opened up to a random page, and the entry said, "Me and Jay had really good intentions to do good this year, but as usual, we really screwed that up." I sat there and thought about how sad it was that there was such a time in my life that I thought it was normal to live such a defeated life. I felt that life was all about the luck of the draw, and I just had no game in me whatsoever. I felt like the world was against me. I felt that the cops were always just profiling me and picking me over everyone else to arrest. I felt like my neighbors were too nosy and that my family cared about too much stuff that was not any of their business. I was living a life where I was constantly trying but never getting anywhere. Like a hamster on a wheel, I was going and going and trying but I was not getting anywhere.

I have grown so much since that time in my life, and I know now that the world is not against me. As a matter of fact, I realize that the world was not against me even then. As I have looked back at all of my past events, I have learned that things were nothing like I had perceived them. God was there all along with His love and mercy, always ready to gently direct me to the path that He had already set out for me. That path that God called me to has been there since before I was born (Galatians 1:15). But it was I who chose not to go on that path. Still, God waited patiently for me to return to Him, just as the parable Jesus told of the prodigal son. We read of this parable in the fifteenth chapter of Luke.

> *Then He said: "A certain man had two sons. And the younger of them said to his father, 'Father, give me the portion of goods that falls to me.' So he divided to them his livelihood. And not many days after, the younger son gathered all together, journeyed to a far country, and there wasted his possessions with prodigal living. But when he had spent all, there arose a severe famine in that land, and he began to be in want. Then he went and joined himself to a citizen of that country, and he sent him into his fields to feed swine. And he would gladly have filled his stomach with the pods that the swine ate, and no one gave him anything. But when he came to himself, he said, 'How many of my father's hired servants have bread enough and to spare, and I perish with hunger! I will arise and go to my father, and will say to him, "Father, I have sinned against heaven and before you, and I am no longer worthy to be called your son. Make me like one of your hired servants."" And he arose and came to his father. But when he was still a great way off, his father saw him and had compassion, and ran and fell on his neck and kissed him. And the son said to him, 'Father, I have sinned against heaven and in your sight, and am no longer worthy to be called your son.' But the father said to his servants, 'Bring out the best robe and put it on him, and put a ring on his hand and sandals on his feet. And bring the fatted calf here and kill it and let us eat and be merry; for this my son was dead and is alive again; he was lost and is found.' And they began to be merry. (Luke 15:11–24)*

The Google dictionary defines "prodigal" as "spending money or resources freely and recklessly; wastefully extravagant." *Merriam-Webster* defines a "prodigal son/daughter" as "a son/daughter who leaves his or her parents to do things that they do not approve of but then feels sorry and returns home." It mentions that it is often used figuratively. Just looking at the definition, you may not feel like the word "prodigal" really pertains to you or your situation. That is how I felt for the longest time but let us dig a little more into the scripture to gain an even deeper understanding. The Holman Christian Standard Bible puts verse 13 this way: "Not many days later, the younger son gathered together all he had and traveled to a distant country, where he squandered his estate in foolish living." In case you did not know "to squander" means to waste something, especially money or time. I do not know about you, but I wasted lots of time and money during my life of drug abuse. Let us look at the Amplified version: "A few days later, the younger son gathered together everything [that he had] and traveled to a distant country, and there he wasted his fortune in reckless and immoral living" (Luke 15:13).

Immoral? That means to not conform to accepted standards of morality. That sounds like half of the things I was involved in during my active addiction. I had heard this story preached many times, and I never doubted in my heart that I had left the Father and I was like the lost son. But for the longest time, I did not realize just how much I was like him. Do you know that we too have a Father in heaven who has given us an inheritance? The whole Bible is full of all that we have inherited through Christ as God's sons and daughters (Ephesians 1:11). We have inherited victory (1 Corinthians 15:57). We have inherited a sure promise that all of our needs will be met (Philippians 4:19). We have inherited direct access to God through the Holy Spirit (Ephesians 2:18) and so much more. God's Word is God's will for our lives, and it is full of blessings and promises that are ours to have. The Word equips us with all we need to live a fulfilled, victorious life of heaven on earth. We also have an inherited promise to live eternally with God the Father once we leave this place. But we do not have to wait until we get to heaven to have His promises fulfilled in our lives.

Although it is quite rude and vain for a person to walk up and say to their parent, "Hey, I know you are still alive, but I think you should just go ahead and give me all that will be mine once you die." I mean, that is basically what the prodigal son had done. His father had not even passed away yet, and nowhere in the scripture does it even indicate that his father was to be passing anytime soon. It just says that the son wanted his inheritance now, and that was bold of him. And if you are like I was, you may be thinking, "Well, that does not pertain to me." But does it? As I have just mentioned, God has already given us access to our inheritance through the word of God. And I am completely certain that I went off and wasted every promise and blessing that the Father had for me by my reckless living. I completely abandoned all of it to go out and live the way I desired and not how I knew I should be living. I lived a way that I knew the Father disapproved of, which is why I purposefully ignored His existence.

That is precisely what the prodigal son did; he went out and spent all that his father had given him on reckless, riotous, immoral living. The scripture says that once he had spent all that he had, there came a severe famine in the land, and he began to be in want. So not only was he broke from spending all the money but the whole land was in lack, which made it even more challenging for him because he had nothing left to his name.

So he became so desperate that he went to work for a citizen of that country and worked in the swine field (not the best of jobs). Then the son became so hungry that it says, "he would gladly have filled his stomach with the pods that the swine ate, and no one gave him anything." The pods that this passage is speaking of are husk-like shells from a carob tree with bean-like seeds inside it. Technically, it was edible to humans, but the point is that the son was so hungry that he envied the pigs' food. When I first studied this, I thought to myself, "Wow, he was desperate to be longing to eat pig food." I mean, thankfully, I have not ever been in a place of starvation, but I felt like it must have been an all-time low for him to have desired pig food.

The word does not say how wealthy his father was, but the fact that his father had enough to even leave him an inheritance in the first place shows that they were well off. He went from being well off in life to being desperate for pig food. I know that I was pretty well off when I started using. I kept a job, fulfilled my responsibilities, and got high on what I could afford. Then before I knew it, I compromised one thing after another until I ended up just like he did. I had spent all of my resources on drugs. Then I was no longer a "responsible" user (if there is even such a thing). The things that I once swore I never would do started to look pleasing, just like the pig food. I would never have imagined to be using drugs while I was participating with my boyfriend in selling them just to pay for our addiction. I would never have imagined that I would be using the money my dad gave me to get me out of the bind I was in with my bills to get high and ignoring the unpaid bills. I would never have imagined living my whole life as one big lie. I would never have imagined being a part of many of the things that I was. As a matter of fact, earlier on in my addiction, most of the things that took place around me looked like "pig food" to me. It looked like slop that I wanted nothing to do with; but eventually, as my addiction progressed and I got desperate enough to continue living my life getting high without any money to do so, certain things stopped looking as bad, and some things even started to look appealing.

Like the prodigal son, the life that I was living was everything short of the fulfillment I had been seeking. The drugs were no longer numbing me to reality like they were in the beginning, and my life was just broken. That was when I finally came to my senses in the passenger seat of my car, and I cried out to my Heavenly Father and told Him that I could not live this way anymore. I knew that I was not living right and that I was not worthy of any favors from Him, but I was at a loss for direction. It was the same way when I called out to Him in the jail cell when I backed myself into a corner, and I had no more hope left in me.

This is exactly what the prodigal son finally came to; he realized that he was living a life that lacked fulfillment and meaning. He realized that if he would just return home, then his father would at least hire him to be a servant, and that way, he would not be starving anymore. The son realized that he was unworthy of forgiveness because of all the things he had done and because of the life he had chosen to live, but if all his father would do was hire him as a servant, it would be better than the life that he was living. So he returned home with that expectation in his heart. But the word says that even while the son was still a great way off, his father saw him and had compassion and ran and fell on his neck and kissed his son. The father was so thankful to see that his son had returned that he did not condemn him. He only rejoiced, and even though all the son wanted was grace enough to be his servant, the father wanted to celebrate because his lost son had come home. There was only love in the father's heart for his son.

When I called out to God in the passenger seat of my car and while lying in my jail cell, this is what my Heavenly Father did. He rejoiced. He came to me and met me right where I was in the lowest part of my life. He is a God of love. He has compassion for us, and He cares for us just as a father cares about a child; He is a better father because God is not human (Numbers 23:19), and He does not make the same mistakes humans make. Therefore, he does not respond as we do. I cried out to God, only needing a way out of the self-induced hell that I was stuck in, but God answered and gave me much more. Even though I still did not submit to immediate deliverance in my life, God never forgot my cry for help, and He was helping me in ways that I did not even know I needed.

My life was never meant for defeat; no one's life is meant for defeat. Our lives were made because God wanted fellowship; He created us so that we could have fellowship with Him, and He has the best life prepared for those who are willing to live it.

"For whosoever shall call upon the name of the Lord shall be saved." Romans 10:13, (KJV)

When I cried out to Him, God started working, and He never gave up on me. I am thankful for His love that carried me through because I had hurt so many people and burned so many bridges in my life, and I felt hopeless because of it. To my self-righteous mindset, every dead-end turn appeared like the world was against me, but I now know it was God turning me away from the life I had been living. He was closing doors that I could not close on my own. While getting arrested each time, I would have a pity party in my mind, thinking, "Why me? What am I doing that is so bad? What about all those who are far worse criminals than I am?" I could not understand why there were so many more people the law should be worried about, such as the big-time drug dealers and those who committed crimes like stealing and whatever else to maintain their addiction. Yet here I was, just a girl who liked to get high. I may lie and take advantage of my family, but I was not a bad person doing bad things to people. But every turn I made, I was catching another drug charge, and I just could not understand the turn of events in every situation I found myself in until I was backed into a corner and given a choice between Drug Court or prison. I was finally put in a place where I was sober, and I was given a chance to get my mind right; after some time, my eyes were finally open to the truth.

The truth was that God had me right where I needed to be. In the strangest way, it was a blessing and not a curse every time I was arrested. It was the answer to my prayer to save me from myself because it was better for me to be in jail than possibly dead somewhere or involved in something I could never have escaped. These things kept happening to me and not to all of those around me who were doing way worse things than I was because I had called out to God, and He was closing the doors to save me. God may have heard me from the beginning; He started the saving process, but He would not force me to surrender to Him fully. God waits for us to surrender to Him because it must be what our hearts desire. If He did it any other way, then it would not be out of real love. It would be like forcing someone to love you. That does not work, and God wants our true love and hearts. It is God's will for all of us to be saved. That is why He is so patient through it all because it is not His will for us to perish into everlasting hell.

> *"The Lord is not slack concerning His promise, as some men count slackness; but is longsuffering to us-ward, not willing that any should perish, but that all should come to repentance."*
> *2 Peter 3:9 (KJV)*

Matthew 23:37 says, "O Jerusalem, Jerusalem, the one who kills the prophets and stones those who are sent to her! How often I wanted to gather your children together, as a hen gathers her chicks under her wings, but you were not willing!" God was speaking through Jesus, saying how many times He just wanted to gather His children together and love them and protect them from the harm they have done to themselves, but they were not willing to let Him. In that same way, I can just imagine all of the times God was willing and ready to cover me and protect me from all the situations I had gotten myself into, but I was never willing to call out to Him or allow His grace to flow through my life. And then there were even moments through His divine mercy and grace when He covered me anyways, but I would just run right out from under the shelter of His wings. For some reason, I always preferred what was killing me inside and out over the love and care of God.

I ran wide open, looking for something to satisfy my heart and to calm my soul. I searched through drugs, alcohol, and relationships to satisfy my soul, and nothing could permanently satisfy me. If I had truly known that what I was searching for to fill my heart and soul was God, then I could have spared myself many heartaches and disappointments. Now that I know that it is God who ultimately fills us and that it was God my soul lacked the entire time, it is the least that I can do to share with you and the entire world that God loves you. If you are searching high and low for something to fill your heart, ask yourself, "Where is God in my life?" You will realize He is either not there at all because you have pushed Him out, or you will find that He is farther from you than He needs to be. When we surrender our heart to God, He will fill it up, and there will be no void. All of your needs will be met through Christ Jesus when you surrender it all to Him.

"But my God shall supply all your need according to His riches in glory by Christ Jesus" Philippians 4:19 (KJV)

Let me go back to comparing our lives to a broken puzzle for a moment. Imagine it is like a children's twelve-piece puzzle that comes put together whenever you buy it. Our life is the puzzle, and it got taken apart. We were whole and undefiled by the world at one time in life, but then the world influenced us and even broke us into pieces. So we started using drugs at some point in our life. For a time, we still have part of our life (or puzzle) intact because we have not made it to complete brokenness. But toward the end of our addiction, piece by piece, our life begins to fall apart. Eventually, some of us have no puzzle pieces together anymore because our lives have been completely pulled apart. Then we come to God and give Him our hearts and our lives, and He begins to put us and our life back together.

But as I mentioned previously, if we do not allow Him to have every area of our hearts and lives, we will never be a whole puzzle. If I come to God and give Him the regrets, the shameful memories, and the mistakes I have made, but I do not allow Him to touch the anger in my heart, I will still have a part of me that is not surrendered to Him. And if I do not surrender it to Him, I still am void of the healing that only He can provide.

I have done many puzzles with my children, and for some reason, they always think that they need to be the one who puts the last piece down; they will sit on that last piece until the puzzle is almost finished. Then when we come to finishing the puzzle, they have to fight over it for completion because neither will hurry and put their piece down. In that same way, that is what our life will look like if we do not allow God to have access to our entire life. Do not sit on certain areas of your heart because you somehow feel you will do a better job at healing it than God can or because you do not like how God is directing your healing. Do not hold onto it because it will only prolong your healing process. Get rid of that void and let God mend you completely and wholly to be used for His glory. The joy of putting together a puzzle is to see its outcome, and in the end, when it is finished, you can enjoy the masterpiece. We should focus on the ultimate goal and just imagine what kind of masterpiece God can build in our lives.

I STRIVE TO MOVE FORWARD

At the time of writing this, I have ten years of sobriety. I am ten years redeemed. I feel like the best way to say it is that I have been a new creation in Christ (2 Corinthians 5:17) for ten years. I feel the words of Apostle Paul in Philippians 3:13–14 best explain where I am in my life right now. "Brethren, I do not count myself to have apprehended; but one thing I do, forgetting those things which are behind and reaching forward to those things which are ahead, I press toward the goal for the prize of the upward call of God in Christ Jesus." I do not feel like I have made it yet. I know that I have so much more to learn about and grow in Christ, and that goes for all of us as we will only be perfected once we make it to heaven. But as far as "addiction" goes, I will in no way say that I am an addict because I have been delivered and redeemed. That was the old me, which is why I said it best fits me to say that I have been a new creation for ten years. If God, the creator of the universe, says I am a new creation and no longer an addict, who am I to keep myself bound by the identity of an addict? I will not look at it like I can use here, there, or on this occasion and not be bound by it either because I now have given my heart and life to Christ, and I must choose to follow Him daily and not the world. I will remember my past, but I will not let it define who I am. So every day, I look forward to growth and reach forward to every new thing that God places before me.

I have maintained my new life in Christ by continuing to do the things that gave me freedom from the beginning. I have a relationship with God, I stay close to Him, and I talk to Him. I seek Him for guidance and direction in my daily life. I diligently search for Him so that I may learn more and more about who God is. It is just like any relationship that we have; it takes effort. Like a husband and wife, they must put in the effort to learn and grow as a couple, or their marriage will fail. If I only talked to my husband once a week and only acknowledged him when I needed help, then our relationship would not be strong. As a matter of fact, it would be weak, we would drift apart, and we would ultimately end up separated if we never made any changes. A relationship takes time and dedication, and it is no different with God.

I stay in His Word, and I make it a priority to read something from it daily. I depend on it to feed my spirit just as I depend on food to feed my physical body. Jesus tells us in Matthew 4:4 (KJV), "But He answered and said, It is written, Man shall not live by bread alone, but by every word that proceedeth out of the mouth of God." The word of God is bread for our spirits; it nourishes us and helps us grow from babies in Christ to who God has called us to be. Just as a baby cannot grow without milk and nourishment, we cannot grow spiritually without the Word to feed us.

I stay in fellowship with other believers who have the same mind and life ambitions as I do. Proverbs 13:20 says, "He who walks with wise men will be wise, But the companion of fools will be destroyed." It is as the saying goes "Birds of a feather flock together." You are about the same business as those you are around. This is not to be judgmental about how other people live, but it is to be smart to stay on the path you have before you.

In the same way that when I started using, I slowly but surely drifted far away from all of the people in my life who did not use. I did it because they were not about the business that I was. I cannot compromise my walk with God by being influenced by sin and ungodly agendas. Twelve-step programs and state rehabs will counsel people by telling them that they must change their people, places, and things. I took this advice wholeheartedly; it is like setting yourself up for failure by attempting to do right and stay sober while you see everyone else around you do the things you are trying to avoid. Even if you have been delivered from drugs, it is not smart to meddle in things that can drag you down. I have seen so many people get it right and even delivered from drugs do well while staying on track and fellowshipping with other believers and seeking God. But then, the moment they stopped attending church regularly and started fellowshipping too much with people from their past, they made faulty choices that quickly helped them to get pulled right back into the bondage of addiction. Apostle Paul says in Galatians 4:9 (HCSB), "But now, since you know God, or rather have become known by God, how can you turn back again to the weak and bankrupt elemental forces? Do you want to be enslaved to them all over again?" In that same way, why would anyone desire to go back to the things that enslaved them once before? Instead, we should stay around those who will encourage us to go in the direction that God is calling us to.

    I keep striving, and I keep growing the best that I can each day. I have days that are better than others, but that is because I am human. One thing that I hold onto each day is the truth spoken in 1 Corinthians 15:57 (KJV): "But thanks be to God, which giveth us the victory through our Lord Jesus Christ." I have victory in Christ Jesus, and I will hold onto that as I face each day. I can rest assured knowing that I am not fighting for victory anymore; instead, as I remain in Jesus, I am fighting from the winning side. In Jesus, I am victorious!

    Today I live in the country with my family of six. After Jake and I got married, we moved to live close to my dad and his farm to start our family. God blessed me with a bonus daughter who was Jake's when we got together, and since then, we have had three more children. I am so thankful for all that God has given our family and for all that he has restored in our lives. We attend church every week, not out of duty but with a thankful and serving heart. Giving my life and its meaning to the Lord is the least I can do for the sacrifice He made for me on the cross. I currently hold faith-based recovery meetings once a week in my community. I do it to be the voice of God for anyone who has court-mandated meetings to attend. I want to minister to others the truth about a real God who can deliver us and set us free from the chains of addiction and make a lasting change in our hearts and lives. I do jail ministry because my heart is for every woman behind bars who may not know the truth. God has given me life and meaning. I praise Him for all that He has done and will continue to do. I pray that whoever you are and wherever you are my testimony can encourage you in some way—whether that is to take a leap of faith and reach out to God or if it is to remind you that we serve a wonderful living God who rescues, redeems, and delivers because our God is an awesome God!

"For with God nothing shall be impossible."
Luke 1:37 (KJV)

CONCLUDING PRAYERS

I have included a salvation prayer for anyone ready to make the life-changing decision. I also have a prayer for codependency and generational curses to help anyone who may not know where to start. I am here to testify that a new life is available for you and healing is possible. Too often, people want change, but no one wants to put forth the work for change. One day I heard the Holy Spirit softly whisper to my heart, "Change does not happen by simply thinking about it; change takes place when one takes action." We must physically do something about our situation and our lives, or nothing will ever be different. Take a leap of faith and see what all God has in store for you.

SALVATION PRAYER

Dear Heavenly Father, I come to you today asking for the forgiveness of my sins. I am tired. My heart and my mind are tired of fighting everything that I keep losing against. I am powerless over _____ in my life, and I need Your help. I confess with my mouth and believe in my heart that Jesus is Your Son and that He died on the cross that I might be forgiven and have eternal life in heaven. I believe that He rose from the grave and is now seated at your right hand. Jesus, I ask you into my heart as my personal Lord and Savior. I ask you to be Lord over my life. I ask you to show me how to live. I pray for the wisdom and strength to move forward from here. Help me, Lord, to turn my life around and live for you in freedom. In Jesus's name, amen.

"That if you confess with your mouth the Lord Jesus and believe in your heart that God has raised Him from the dead, you will be saved. For with the heart one believes unto righteousness, and with the mouth confession is made unto salvation. For the Scripture says, 'Whoever believes on Him will not be put to shame'" (Romans 10:9–11).

"Which He worked in Christ when He raised Him from the dead and seated him at His right hand in the heavenly places."
Ephesians 1:20

If we confess our sins, He is faithful and just to forgive us our sins and to cleanse us from all unrighteousness."
1 John 1:9

PRAYER TO BE DELIVERED FROM CODEPENDENCY

As you can see from my testimony, codependency was a big part of my past. I was always searching for a way for other people to fulfill me and my heart's void, along with my search for fulfillment through drugs. I am including a prayer for anyone who may have the same struggle that I had because ultimately God desires that we be set free from anything and all things that keep us from being fulfilled through Him. God's will for us is to find our identity, love, and affirmation from Him and Him alone.

God, I come before you today, and I repent of looking toward other people and things to fulfill my heart when you have created me to be fulfilled by You. I ask You to deliver me from the mindset that I need another person to feel whole. I come to You today, and I ask You for the strength and ability to overcome the mentality of needing a person's approval and love to feel complete. I desire You to be my heart and for You to be the One who fills the void in my life, so God, I ask that Your love would overwhelm me in such a powerful way that I know without a doubt that You and You alone are my fulfillment. I ask for Your mercy and grace to strengthen me as

I continuously learn to seek You and Your Kingdom first so that all else in my life will stem from it daily. In Jesus's name, amen.

GENERATIONAL CURSES

For this commandment which I command you today is not too mysterious for you, nor is it far off. It is not in heaven, that you should say, "Who will ascend into heaven for us and bring it to us, that we may hear it and do it?" Nor is it beyond the sea, that you should say, "Who will go over the sea for us and bring it to us, that we may hear it and do it?" But the word is very near you, in your mouth and in your heart, that you may do it. See, I have set before you today life and good, death and evil, in that I command you today to love the Lord your God, to walk in His ways, and to keep His commandments, His statutes, and His judgments, that you may live and multiply; and the Lord your God will bless you in the land which you go to possess. But if your heart turns away so that you do not hear, and are drawn away, and worship other gods and serve them, I announce to you today that you shall surely perish; you shall not prolong your days in the land which you cross over the Jordon to go in and possess. I call heaven and earth as witnesses today against you, that I have set before you life and death, blessing and cursing; therefore choose life, that both you and your descendants may live; that you may love the Lord your God, that you may obey His voice, and that you may cling to Him, for he is your life and the length of your days; and that you may dwell in the land which the Lord swore to your fathers, to Abraham, Isaac, and Jacob, to give them." (Deuteronomy 30:11–20)

When God delivered His children, the Israelites, out of Egypt and promised to bring them into their promised land, He assured them that He would bless them, protect them, and take care of them as long as they were obedient to Him and His commands. But if they chose to go after other gods and did not obey Him and His commandments, there would be curses upon them for their disobedience. You can read in more depth about the blessings or curses in Deuteronomy chapter 28. But just as the Israelites were facing the next step to possess their promised land, God spoke these scriptures that I just mentioned earlier as a reminder of what He had already told them in Deuteronomy 28. God was and is now telling His people (including you and me) how it is not hard for us to find or understand what He is saying. And that we all have a choice between life and death and between blessing and cursing. God did not make it some big mystery that only a few can figure out; He has made it plain and simple for all to understand. It was simple then and is just as simple today because God and His word does not change (Psalm. 33:11, Isaiah 40:8, Malachi 3:6).

So today, we have a choice to love the Lord and walk in His ways and then be blessed because of it, or we can choose to live our lives our own way, serve other gods, and live not in the blessings of God but in curses. When we live in sin and choose the lifestyle of drug abuse, we open doors of curses upon our lives. Thus, by opening the doors of curses into our lives, it opens the doors upon our children's lives. Maybe we were raised in a home of addiction, and we are not the first in our family to live this life. In either case, we have inherited a generational curse or exposed our children to the lifestyle and opened the door to a generational curse within our bloodline. If we do not have children, we can still choose to stop the cycle of addiction and receive deliverance.

In my family, my mom was an addict, and her father was an alcoholic. Out of my mom's children, I was the only one who went down that path, but it had stemmed down to the third generation before it was stopped. I cannot speak for you, but you can see what I am saying if you take a moment to look back. Think back on your life and figure out where it all started. Maybe it was with you, or perhaps it was with your parents or even their parents. Or if this does not pertain to you and your family, take a moment and think back to other people you have known (not to judge but just to observe and understand what I am saying). You can see how addiction has been passed down in the family for multiple generations in some families. This is because a generational curse can be passed down from one generation to another due to rebellion against God. Addiction can remain within families who have known nothing but that lifestyle, and then they teach it to their children, who teach it to their children. That is because generational curses come from learned behavior from within the lived-in and taught environment.

> *"Keeping mercy for thousands, forgiving iniquity and transgression and sin, by no means clearing the guilty, visiting the iniquity of the fathers upon the children and the children's children to the third and the fourth generation."*
> *Exodus 34:7*

The Word of God says that God visits the iniquity of the fathers upon the children up to four generations. According to *Merriam-Webster*, iniquity is gross injustice, wickedness; a wicked act; or sin. I am not saying that all children in the bloodline of an addict are doomed or cursed because God also states in His word that the children are not guilty just because of the parent's sin (Ezekiel 18:20), so please hear what I am saying. The parents' lifestyle of iniquity can open the door to a generational curse in the family. As the children live the lives that the parents taught them, their lives of iniquity can continue to further generations. Looking at the bigger picture, the fact of the matter is this: we are a slave of sin until we are set free by the redemptive work of Jesus Christ (Romans 6:20–23). And until one learns this, the behavior and lifestyle will continue, and it may pass from generation to generation.

But once we come to the truth, which is that salvation and repentance will set us free from the bondage of sin, we can be set free and then start a new cycle for our lives and our children's lives—a cycle of living for God, walking in His ways, and keeping His commandments so that we are living in His promised blessings. Even if you do not have children, this can still pertain to you as you have to decide whether or not you desire lasting deliverance from the bondage of addiction. You can still choose today to turn your heart and your life to God and turn your cycle of searching for fulfillment through drugs into a cycle of living in fulfillment through Christ because Christ has come to set us free!

"For God so loved the world that He gave His only begotten Son, that whoever believes in Him should not perish but have everlasting life. For God did not send His Son into the world to condemn the world, but that the world through Him might be saved."
John 3:16–17

"Jesus answered them, 'Most assuredly, I say to you, whoever commits sin is a slave of sin. And a slave does not abide in the house forever, but a son abides forever. Therefore if the Son makes you free, you shall be free indeed.'" John 8:34–36

"If we confess our sins, He is faithful and just to forgive us our sins and to cleanse us from all unrighteousness."
1 John 1:9

As we come to know Jesus as our personal Lord and Savior and as we confess our sins, they are washed away, and we can have a new beginning. And in God's eyes, our slates are wiped clean, but we should do our part in stepping out of the world that we had been involved in for so long. We need to be ready and willing to break all ties with our past physically and spiritually. We need to be ready and willing to allow God to work in us toward changing our behavior for the good of Him through us. This is a place in our hearts where we stand up and say, "Addiction stops with me!" You can take a stand to stop the curse of addiction in your life so that *you* do not pass it on to *your* children's lives by saying, "Addiction stops at my bloodline! And living to serve the Lord starts with my bloodline here and now, in the name of Jesus!" By saying a prayer for God not only to stop but to put an end to curses in your bloodline that have previously been a part of your life due to your own choices and actions, you are asking God to fight the spiritual side of the battle that you cannot fight in your strength.

STEPS TOWARD FREEDOM

The first step to true freedom is accepting Jesus Christ into your heart as your personal Lord and Savior. Then you must confess your sins to God and ask Him for forgiveness so that you may come before Him with a clean heart. Then you can begin asking God to cut off all bad roots from your family tree. Just like if we were cutting down a tree that we did not want on our property, we must cut off the root of the tree or else it will not completely die. If we did not cut it at its roots, it would spring back up one day, whether that would be in our lifetime or our children's lifetime. So to have complete freedom from any generational curses that you may be in or have opened, ask God to lay the axe to every evil root within your bloodline.

PRAYER OF DELIVERANCE

God, I come to you in the name of Jesus, and I ask you for the forgiveness of my sins and the sins of my family. I confess my sins to you today, and I repent of them. I desire to live a new life in You through Your Son Jesus. I ask that you forgive the sins from my mother's bloodline and my father's bloodline, four generations back, the sins that they have committed, whether knowingly or unknowingly. I know that Jesus has come and paid the ultimate price for my salvation and freedom, and I come to claim my freedom through Christ today. I speak with the authority that Christ has given me. I command the roots of these curses that have engrafted themselves to my family and me be uprooted and destroyed in the same way that Jesus spoke words against the fig tree in *Matthew 21:19–20* and that tree withered up and died. God, I pray that through Your glory, power, and mighty hand You would lay an axe to every bad root in my life and bloodline. I receive Your deliverance and freedom today, and I ask that You continue to open my eyes daily to You and Your Word so that I may continue to grow and be led to the path of Your righteousness. In Jesus's name, amen.

If you would like to contact the author you can email her at whenchainsarebroken@gmail.com

If you would like help share this testimony and donate a book for those who are fighting this battle, incarcerated, or in rehabilitation centers please contact the author.

CPSIA information can be obtained
at www.ICGtesting.com
Printed in the USA
LVHW050901160222
711266LV00012B/869